Debt-Proof
Your
Christmas

Other books by Mary Hunt

7 Money Rules for Life
Raising Financially Confident Kids

Debt–Proof Your Christmas

Celebrating the Holidays without Breaking the Bank

Mary Hunt

Revell

a division of Baker Publishing Group
Grand Rapids, Michigan

Published by Revell
a division of Baker Publishing Group
P.O. Box 6287, Grand Rapids, MI 49516-6287
www.revellbooks.com

Printed in the United States of America

Library of Congress Cataloging-in-Publication Data
Hunt, Mary, 1948–
    Debt-proof your Christmas : celebrating the holidays without breaking the bank / Mary Hunt.
        p.   cm.
    Includes bibliographical references (p.   ) and index.
    ISBN 978-0-8007-2143-5 (pbk.)
    1. Finance, Personal. 2. Christmas. 3. Holidays. I. Title.
HG179.H85486 2012
332.024'02—dc23   2012013517

Published in association with The Steve Laube Agency, 5025 N. Central Ave., #635, Phoenix, Arizona 85012-1502.

The internet addresses, email addresses, and phone numbers in this book are accurate at the time of publication. They are provided as a resource. Baker Publishing Group does not endorse them or vouch for their content or permanence.

In keeping with biblical principles of creation stewardship, Baker Publishing Group advocates the responsible use of our natural resources. As a member of the Green Press Initiative, our company uses recycled paper when possible. The text paper of this book is composed in part of post-consumer waste.

green press
INITIATIVE

12   13   14   15   16   17   18   7   6   5   4   3   2   1

To
my friend
Kathleen Chapman,
a woman of many talents,
not the least of which is the
ability to take a pile of empty
Jell-O boxes, scraps of paper, curling
ribbon, and a few twinkle lights and produce a
Christmas tree
so elegant
it defies
description

Contents

A Note from the Author

This is a book about special holidays and debt. Because I celebrate Christmas, you will see many references to this holiday. But if you celebrate Hanukkah, Kwanzaa, or some other special holiday, these same principles, ideas, and suggestions can apply. Just make your holiday substitution each time you come to the word *Christmas*.

All references to debt in this book are to unsecured debt such as revolving credit-card balances, installment loans, and personal loans. Debt, as it is used in this book, does not refer to secured debt such as mortgages or auto loans.

Acknowledgments

I owe a debt of gratitude to the many Debt-Proof Living readers who over the years have generously shared their best Christmas memories, tips, and gift ideas and graciously allowed me to share them with you.

I offer my heartfelt appreciation and thanks to the Revell team for welcoming the idea of this book and to my editor, Vicki Crumpton, for piloting the process to publication.

Many thanks to Cathy Hollenbeck and the rest of my Debt-Proof Living staff for all they do on a daily basis to keep me pointed in the right direction and moving forward.

Last, to the most important people in my life—my family—thanks for cheering me on and giving me the space I need to write. But more than that, thanks for giving me a reason to get all excited about Christmas, year after year. The memories of all the good times we've had through the years are tucked in my heart forever.

Introduction

It was my worst Christmas ever. I'd been hiding bills from my husband so we would have money for Christmas shopping, but it wasn't enough. It never was.

Every credit card in my vast collection was maxed to the limit. Back then going over limit was not allowed. If you tried, the card would be rejected at the cash register. There are few things more humiliating than the dreaded words, "You'll need to go to the credit office."

With only seven days to go until the big day, I was desperate. Still to come were parties, school events, church pageants, and musicals. The pressure of the season was taking its toll. The stress was nearly unbearable.

I did the only thing I could do: I called the department stores whose cards I had and begged for a credit limit increase. One high-end store agreed. That determined my course of action. I would have to Christmas shop in a big chichi store that specialized in clothing.

The store directory assured me it had toys and electronics too. But just try to find them. When I did find toys and electronics, the selections were limited and the prices outlandish. But by then I didn't care what the price tags read. There was so little time left, and I was determined to mark the last names off my list and just get this shopping thing finished.

Before I go on, you need to know this was quite a few years ago when VCRs (videocassette recorders) were fairly new technology and quite the buzz. I purchased a VCR from that department store for my husband. It cost more than six hundred dollars—about double what they were going for at the time in discount electronics stores. But what were my other choices? My only available credit was at this one department store.

I tore through that increased credit limit in no time flat. I bought toys and clothes and of course the pricey VCR. The kids weren't impressed; neither was my husband. He couldn't quite understand my choice of gifts because we already had a VCR. Not a very good one, I pointed out.

I don't remember much else from that miserable Christmas. If there was any joy or satisfaction, it was lost in the shadow of the frantic last-minute shopping and all the debt I added to an already out-of-control situation. Of course, the regular bills couldn't hide forever, and their reappearance in the New Year did not endear me to my husband. Add to them the bills for all that Christmas shopping and you'll have a small idea of the angst and disharmony in the Hunt household.

I'm certain we paid for that VCR at least three times by the time we finally got out of debt many years later. The debt lasted far longer than the machine, which has long since gone to the big electronic graveyard in the sky. But it remains for me an important symbol of what not to do.

After that low point of my life, I made a U-turn on the road to financial devastation. It took nearly thirteen years to repay all the horrible debt I had amassed (a story for another day), but the important thing is that we did it. We paid back a six-figure load of unsecured debt, and in the process, it changed our lives.

If there's one thing I learned from that Christmas so many years ago, it is this: Stuff quickly fades, but debt goes on and on.

As you read this now, it may be spring or fall. As I write, it's summer. The days are long, the grass is green, and the livin' is easy. Even so, and no matter what time of year it is, there is something we need to talk about. Relatively speaking, the holidays are just a few short months away. Christmas can creep up on us like a swimsuit that's a couple of sizes too small.

I don't know how much credit-card debt has your name on it, but the fact that you're reading this book suggests there might be some. Or perhaps you aren't in debt, but you want to make sure you stay that way. There's no doubt that relying on credit to pay for holiday shopping can be very tempting. The credit-card companies want us to believe it won't make any difference—that holiday debt is simple to pay off. But we know better. It's time to say enough is enough.

Being sick and tired of overspending and starting each New Year with a holiday debt hangover for stuff no one remembers is the catalyst that can make things different for you in the future. You have to say, "Enough! I'm not going to do that anymore."

What you hold in your hand is not a challenge to stop giving gifts or celebrating Christmas or even spending money. Not at all. Because every situation is different and there is no one-size-fits-all holiday plan, this book is packed with ideas for how to have an all-cash Christmas. No matter how much or how little cash you have to spend, staying away from credit-card debt is going to change your holiday experience in ways you never dreamed possible.

Here's my challenge for you: This Christmas, lock up the credit cards and let me show you how to experience the best Christmas ever with no debt, less stress, and more joy! I will provide the information and you provide the commitment. We're going to make a great team, so let's get going.

Prepare yourself for the most meaningful Christmas you and your family have ever experienced—a very merry, debt-free Christmas.

"In our fantasies, Christmas comes as a beautiful horse-drawn sleigh to carry us gently through the season. But in reality, Christmas comes at us like an eighteen-wheeled, supercharged, nitrous-burning, straight-six, diesel-powered, self-propelled juggernaut of a big rig."

1

Christmas—Back by Popular Demand

I love Christmas. I mean I *really* love Christmas. And if you're anything like me—somehow I have a feeling that might be the case—it's the fondness for the holiday that can so easily get us into difficulty.

The trouble with Christmas is that we allow the overcommercialization of the season to get the better of us. We get caught up in the man-made hype and treat Christmas as a popularity contest or final examination rather than a time of rest, reflection, and joy.

In our fantasies, Christmas comes as a beautiful horse-drawn sleigh to carry us gently through the season to the sounds of the clippety-clop of horses' hooves and the jingling of sleigh bells. We visit friends and loved ones, exchange lovely tokens of our love and esteem for one another, and indulge in warm and meaningful conversations. Our grateful children frolic in the snow, amazed at the generosity of their parents.

But in reality, Christmas comes at us like an eighteen-wheeled, super-charged, nitrous-burning, straight-six, diesel-powered, self-propelled juggernaut of a big rig fueled by consumer credit, and lots of it. It screams for us to get on board.

The thirty or so days between Thanksgiving and Christmas become a blur as we tear through the season, feeling obligated to stop at every turn to decorate, shop, clean, cook, bake, wrap, and send. The rig is programmed to go faster and faster because there is so little time and so many miles to cover before the journey's end.

This machine needs fuel—and credit cards are the combustible of choice. We are terrified at how often we need to refuel.

With so many mandatory parties, pageants, and projects, we find little time to sleep. We feel ourselves being consumed by guilt and obligation, so we try to counteract those feelings by charging (please let it be deferred billing) bigger and better gifts and buying the approval and adoration of everyone on our list. The only thing that matters is getting to the finish line by Christmas Eve. We arrive worn-out and disappointed.

Credit Changed Everything

No doubt about it, celebrating Christmas now is a far cry from what it was even thirty years ago, thanks to the evolution and escalation of consumer credit. No longer must we concern ourselves with whether there's enough money to buy and do all that our hearts desire. Credit-card companies have made it quite socially acceptable to have it all whether we can afford it or not. Little by little, we've allowed ourselves to have what we want now and worry about paying for it later.

The more we have, the more we want; the more we get, the more we need to feel satisfied. It seems that no matter how fantastic Christmas was last year, we are compelled by merchants to make it even bigger and better this year.

When it's all said and done, it seems the gift-giving—which is what really started all of this in the first place—has become all but divorced from the actual impulse, from the love or the kindness. It's just shopping; it's just money; it's crossing names off lists and moving on.

But it doesn't have to be that way. You can decide right now that Christmas for you and your family will not be dictated by the retail industry, which has its sights on your wallet and your wealth.

Selective Amnesia

Here's the problem. We live eleven months of the year as if Christmas will never come again, then we go into a panic when it does—concluding that we have no choice but to put everything on the credit cards "just this one last time." And then it happens over and over again.

Blame it on what I call selective amnesia. People who suffer from this condition fall into some kind of seasonal coma. They block Christmas from their minds until it's too late to plan ahead. And it's little wonder. For many, Christmas is no longer the most blessed but rather the most stressful time of the year. And expensive. But somehow we all manage to get through it, many with a pile of new debt and a solemn vow to start earlier next year. We just don't want to think about it.

If your resolve lapses into unconsciousness somewhere around Valentine's Day, how grateful you must be that I'm here to jolt you back to reality.

Predict and Prepare

So you may be asking, "Is there an antidote for this condition?"

The answer is yes, and it can be found in these two words: *predict* and *prepare*.

Predicting is the easy part. If you can read a calendar, you've got this nailed. Christmas is never early, never late. You always know exactly when it will arrive. The trick is to stay focused on where you are in relation to December 25, both chronologically and financially.

Preparing is another story. There are probably as many variables that play into preparing for Christmas as there are personalities and financial situations. There is no one-size-fits-all solution. Finding a plan that fits your financial condition, your family situation, and your comfort zone is the key.

Perhaps you're the type who finds early Christmas shopping and preparation to be counterproductive. You overbuy. Or you second-guess yourself. What seems perfect in July is all wrong come December. You can't get creative or excited about the holidays until the season arrives. Besides, you're not crafty, so making gifts is out of the question. The way you need to prepare is to begin stashing cash now to fund your famous two-day blitz when you will get everything done start to finish.

If, on the other hand, you are a quintessential plan-ahead soul with crafter's blood coursing through your veins, you cannot imagine choosing to wait until the last minute. And if forced into that position by financial constraints, you're a basket case just waiting to happen. You're ready to get started when you finish reading this.

Compelled to Get It Right

There were many years when I saw Christmas as a final exam. I had to get it right because there would be no do-overs. Whatever felt good, whatever the kids wanted and others expected—that's what I did. And when it was over, it wasn't really over. I limped my way into each New Year suffering from a horrible hangover of new debt piled on top of the old. Month after month, the ghost of Christmas past haunted me with bills that lasted much longer than the stuff I had bought.

The sense of urgency and bright lights of the season can trick us into believing we are Christmas magicians, that by some miracle we can do it all and easily pay for it later. Let's turn down those lights right now. You don't have to give in to those urges. You can choose to approach the season with realistic expectations and a plan, so you can enjoy all the season has to offer and still step into the New Year knowing that everything is paid in full.

Think This Through

While you may be tempted to jump right into creating a gift list, that's not the place to start. Back up another step. What do you want this year's holidays to look like? If you want to experience a warm and meaningful time with family and friends, pouring all of your resources into gifts may not be the best way to accomplish that.

The way to control your holiday spending is to come up with a plan. If past Christmases have left you in debt and less than satisfied, now's the time to start strategizing while your past financial fumbles are fresh in your mind—and the next holiday season is some distance in the future.

You know what they say about hindsight being 20/20. Your fuzzy vision becomes frighteningly clear around January 15, when all the holiday bills start rolling in and you lock eyeballs with your ATM withdrawals—crumpled receipts stuffed in your wallet—now all neatly lined up on your bank statement for review.

Here is the painful truth: A little bit here, a lot more there—it all adds up. Rather than wonder about and weep over all the money you spent, determine that you will not allow your emotions to spark a repeat performance. Plan to do better next year.

What Was I Thinking?

I'll never forget the year I had a very ambitious idea to host a Christmas boutique in our home. I've always enjoyed crafts, and the thought of turning our house into a little country store for one weekend in early December sounded like a lot of fun. With any luck I'd end up with enough cash to pay for Christmas.

I invited a few friends to participate, and the word traveled quickly. Before I knew it, I had fifteen participants.

From the moment I decided to go through with this quasi-commercial venture, I became obsessed with the details. Because of the sheer volume of merchandise that would be showing up, I decided to relocate our furniture to the garage and basically move out of the greater portion of our house.

I'm told the event was quite a hit. People lined up around the block long before opening time on the first morning. During the four-day affair, hundreds of people patronized my boutique.

While the entire event remains mostly a blur, I do know that I overplanned, overprepared, overworked, overspent, and overexpected. Basically, I made a fool of myself.

By the time I settled up with all of the selling participants and accounted for all the time and money I had spent on advertising, I ended up with precious little profit.

My clearest memory of the event is that it ruined my life because I went way overboard. It took months to put the house back together, and I still feel the pangs of boutique burnout.

Never once did I consider repeating the idea, and that's a shame, because it was quite successful. Had I taken the time to systematically analyze what I did wrong, what I did right, what I could do to fix the wrongs and repeat the rights, there is an excellent possibility I could have salvaged the idea and turned it into a seasonal cottage industry.

Most of us don't have the option of giving up on Christmas the way I threw out my boutique, nor would we want to. That's why evaluation is important in taking back control.

Consider the Past

As you go through the exercise of considering your Christmases past, don't let guilt and fear enter the picture. Think of yourself as a paid consultant who has been brought into a corporation to look at ways to make the company more efficient and more profitable.

What factors have caused you to overspend in years past? Possibilities may include gift-giving, entertaining, decorating, guilt, peer pressure, family pressure, influence of media (remember that gingerbread village on the magazine cover that looked so cute and was supposed to be easy enough to complete in just one evening?), wanting to make Christmas perfect for your children, attempting to re-create your own childhood, trying to compensate for an absent parent, or waiting until the last minute.

As you look back on previous Christmases, what do you wish you would have done more? Spent time with the kids, played games, put together a puzzle, relaxed, spent time with your spouse, spent time with friends and neighbors, slept, sat in front of the fire and read an entire book, watched *It's a Wonderful Life* all the way through, attended church services and sang all of your favorite Christmas carols, taken a trip into the city just to soak up the sights, taken gifts to the kids at the shelter.

What do you wish you would have done less? Mindless shopping, pageant directing, play producing, party planning, baking, cleaning, cooking, shopping, float building, card writing, worrying, decorating, running around, meeting others' expectations, traveling on Christmas Eve and Christmas Day just to keep everyone else happy.

In what ways are you still paying for the efforts of last Christmas? Credit-card bills, installment loans, soured relationships, wounded spirits, burnout, embarrassment, gifts promised but as yet unfinished or unfulfilled.

What changes are you willing to make starting right now to affect a different outcome this year? As we head into this most wonderful time of the year, you'll be making lots of decisions on how you will use your time and your money. In fact, they may already be coming at you with full force. It takes a lot of courage to go against the flow, but it will be easier if you keep one eye on December 26. See every decision and spending opportunity in the light of what will remain when it's over for another year.

What Really Matters

One year I asked my family of Debt-Proof Living members at Debt ProofLiving.com to tell me about their best Christmas gift ever. I got every kind of response you could possibly imagine. And they were as unique as the individuals who responded. Yet every response had a deep, emotional dimension: spending time with family, welcoming a new family member, surprising loved ones with a visit, receiving a treasured possession from a grandparent. What I learned (I'll be sharing the responses in coming chapters) is that all of the trouble we put ourselves through to spend enough money to be acceptable is often wasted. What really matters is rarely available for purchase in a store.

Whatever your personality or the scope of your goals, the secret to your success will be found in your ability to stick with your plan. The bottom line is that you want to bring wonderful memories and renewed relationships with you into the New Year—not a pile of new debt for all kinds of stuff you can scarcely recall buying.

Remember, it is not up to you to find the absolutely perfect gift that will fulfill the deepest desire of every person on your list. It's not your responsibility to become a mind reader and a dream fulfiller. The people on your list—as much as they love and adore you—probably don't remember what you gave them last year. In the end, it just doesn't matter that much what presents you give, provided that your desired sentiment is conveyed.

So before you get caught up in the emotion of the season and sidetracked by all those offers of "zero interest until next year!" determine how much cash you have to spend. Compare that to the number of gifts you'd like to give and other expenses of the season. Set a dollar limit for each one and stick to it no matter what.

Doing whatever it takes to enjoy an all-cash Christmas is the very best gift you can give yourself and your family.

I know you can do it too.

One year when _Jurassic Park_ was all the rage, my son had only one item on his Christmas list—a jeep-like vehicle that ran by remote control and squirted water from a captured reptile's mouth. The worst part about this request was that it was made early in December, well after the shopping rush of Thanksgiving holiday sales. Online ordering was not my forte at the time, so I searched on foot at every toy store in a fifty-mile radius. The process was so mentally, physically, emotionally, and spiritually draining (because by then I had lost all the meaning of Christmas giving) that my husband and I vowed never to do that again. We put the worst behind us.

The following year I set a limit on purchases and came up with a fantastic idea that to this day my teenage boys continue to enjoy. I purchased two or three "special" items from their list of ten requests with the understanding that they may or may not get the "only thing I ever really wanted!"

What makes this tradition fun is that each gift is wrapped and hidden and the boys are given a clue where to find it. I have even made treasure maps and sent them out into the yard with a shovel! Nothing is more amusing than to have children squealing with delight on Christmas morning as they rummage through the house and yard searching for their gifts. It has provided us with the best feelings of excitement, creativity, and appreciation.

The boys are now fourteen and eighteen and still request that clues be placed in their Christmas stockings.

Amy S., Florida

2

Shaping Your Attitude

Pulling off an all-cash Christmas in the face of a credit-aggressive retail industry is going to be like holding back the sea unless you arm yourself with a very important tool. You won't have to run out and buy this tool, because I am absolutely sure you have it already. And you won't have to go on a whole-house search to find it either. This all-important tool is as close to a magic wand as you will ever get and as powerful as you choose for it to be. It is your attitude.

Your attitude—the way you respond to everything in life—is more important than anything else as you set out to develop an all-cash Christmas. You choose your attitude, your thoughts, and the way you respond to everything that happens around you. How you celebrate and how you pay for the Christmas holidays are completely in your control if you make that choice.

Your attitude is like a child. It can be mature, well-behaved, and responsible, or it can be an out-of-control spoiled brat prone to loud demands and temper tantrums. You may know a little something about that. I know I do. Disciplining my attitude is a full-time job. Some days are easier than others. But consistent self-discipline in choosing my thoughts and what I allow myself to focus on does get easier, because my thinking becomes a habit.

You can choose a joyful, expectant, can-do attitude with bold determination, an attitude that says, "No matter what, I am not going to spend money I do not have to pay for Christmas. Period." With that kind of attitude, even the powerful consumer-credit and retail industries will be no match for you. You will prevail. But if you fail to make that specific decision, you could easily default into debt, because let's face it, buying everything on credit is a lot easier. Not thinking about prices and just spending your brains out with plastic are nearly effortless. What you must keep front and center in your mind is that while it may be easier for a moment, the struggle comes later in the crushing weight of debt.

The Joy and the Work

There are two distinct aspects of Christmas: what we feel and what we do. Both the feeling and the doing are important, and neither part should be denied.

On the one hand, there's the joy of the season that touches our emotions and satisfies our souls. This is the part we feel, the part that evokes memories and binds families together. It's the joy, the wonder—the miracle of the Christ child coming to earth to bring hope to a fallen world. This is the part of Christmas that we feel, the aspect that we approach with our hearts and feel in our spirits.

The other side of the season is the work. It's the business, the planning, and the funding. This side of Christmas you must approach with your head—your good sense, your sound money principles, and your core values, which are grounded in your belief system.

Remember Ebenezer Scrooge of Charles Dickens's *A Christmas Carol*? Before his life-changing encounters with ghosts, it seemed he had no heart. His entire approach to Christmas was cerebral—not a single emotion could be found in his crusty, hardened self. Of course, that is not the proper approach to Christmas. But neither is an all-out emotional onslaught. There has to be balance. And the wise person knows how to move easily between the emotions and the business of Christmas.

That Important Separation

The more successful you are at separating these two aspects of Christmas, the more likely you will come through the holidays without creating debt. And the best "separator" is time.

It's so much easier to set your holiday spending limit when you are not under the emotional spell of the season. You can think more clearly when you are not face-to-face with silver bells and boughs of holly. When you are not emotionally engaged in Christmas is a good time to make specific statements that reflect your chosen holiday attitudes.

Wait until the last minute to start thinking about this and it's easy to get everything mixed up. Before you know it, you'll get sucked into the mind-set that you have to spend a lot of money to create good memories so that everyone will be fully satisfied.

If Christmas is dangerously close as you read this, don't assume you're out of luck to make things different this year. Get away to a quiet place where you can think clearly. Then remember that it's only too late if you don't start now.

A Little Talking To

I know what it's like to think that if we can just spend enough—if we can just get the biggest and best gifts for everyone on our lists—somehow we'll be able to create the kind of joy our hearts crave. It's easy to get caught up in that kind of thinking, but it's not at all true. Approaching the business side of Christmas now while we can think clearly is just so much easier, financially safer, and more effective.

Separating the emotion from the business of Christmas will free you to create a plan and then stick to it—and also enjoy the warmth and wonder of the season to your soul's content.

Here are the kinds of self-talk and personal affirmations you need handy as you formulate your attitudes. Write them on a card and keep them close so you can refer to them often. Of course, these are my suggestions; you may have others to add or substitute that are unique to you.

No one can force me to spend money I do not have in order to pay for Christmas. No one. If I feel pressure to do that and then cave in, it is my fault. I am the one who did the forcing.

The best memories and the most joy come from things money cannot buy.

I will spend my time well, investing myself in my children and others who mean the world to me.

I will keep one eye on December 26, when I intend to wake up knowing Christmas is paid in full.

It is good for children to yearn and to have pre-set boundaries when it comes to wish lists and desires.

Overindulging children is just plain wrong, so I will not do it. I will help them learn to limit their expectations rather than attempt to fulfill their every desire.

I am not a Christmas magician.

I will not work so hard during the month of December that Christmas turns into one crazy blur with "Just let this be over!" written all over it.

I will create my own agenda and not allow retail marketers to do it for me.

Debt Is a Choice

While the credit-card companies and retailers have come up with amazing marketing campaigns that border on mind control, so far they have not figured out how to force us to spend money we do not have. Going into debt is still a choice. And so is not going into debt by opting for an all-cash Christmas.

If your spending habits are nudging you into holiday debt, you don't have to give in. You can experience a joyful season without mortgaging your future in order to feel good. Remember, it's all a matter of attitude. You are in control.

It may seem completely ridiculous to think that just by changing your attitude you can change your circumstance, but it's true.

Disadvantages can be turned into advantages simply by the way you look at them. The happiest people don't necessarily have the best of everything; they just make the best of everything.

Feelings and Actions

Here is a life principle that will help you understand and make meaningful attitude changes: It's easier to act your way into a feeling than to feel your way into an action. If you change your attitude—not because you feel like it but because you know it is the right thing to do—your feelings will follow. On the other hand, if you wait until you "feel like it," meaningful change may be delayed indefinitely.

It is dangerous to allow your life to be guided by feelings. Feelings are fickle—they cannot be trusted. Not only is it foolish to make choices and decisions by the "if it feels good do it" method, but it can also be costly.

And, of course, while we'd like to, it's difficult to ignore the negative feelings of worry, stress, and disappointment; the fear of not doing everything well enough; the envy of those who do more and do it better; and the guilt of not measuring up, not giving the right gift, or not spending enough to even the score.

Christmas can be one overwhelming feeling after another. If we allow our spending to be controlled by our feelings, we're in for a roller-coaster ride that carries a heavy price tag.

Stop allowing your attitudes to be shaped by those feelings brought on by the sights, sounds, and smells of Christmas; by shopping malls, magazines, neighbors, friends, family, or any other person, place, or thing. Instead, shape your attitudes about Christmas and debt in a reasoned and logical manner. You can take care of business and also fully enjoy and engage in the warmth and wonder of the season.

One Christmas many years ago, money was very tight. On Christmas Eve we took the kids out driving to look at the Christmas lights. On the way back we stopped in a five-and-dime variety store. We were having fun just looking and wandering through the aisles when I saw a little nativity set in a small box for eighty-nine cents. My husband offered to get it for me for Christmas, but I felt like there would be better uses for eighty-nine cents. We discussed it a bit, and he bought it. The same year my nine-year-old bought me a Santa candle.

I can't explain why, but I remember vividly that Christmas and those two gifts more than any other. I keep that small nativity piece with Mary, Joseph, and the Christ child on display all year. Every time I see the nativity, I remember that there is something ephemeral about certain times and that money is not the central factor in those special memories.

The ensuing years have been filled with some good, some bad, some happy, some sad times; some financially desperate times; some times when money was in plentiful supply—but all have been sprinkled with unique and special little memories that stand out for reasons I can't always explain.

When I stew and worry and lie awake at night worrying about money or other problems, it really helps to look at my nativity and remember that hope is found in a Person, not in my pocketbook.

Charlotte T., Kansas

Recardulation: Figuring out that by regifting the gift cards you received last year to everyone on your list this year your Christmas shopping is done. And it's only July!

3

Developing a Plan

You probably would not add a family room to your home without a blueprint, knit a sweater without a pattern, or head off on a cross-country vacation without a map. But when it comes to preparing for Christmas, most of us hit the ground running the day after Thanksgiving—without a blueprint, pattern, or map. We get caught up in all the emotion of the season, and before we know it, we're taking Christmas three stairs at a time.

Oh, I know you probably have a gift list—all of us have one of those, and it gives the illusion of a plan—but, believe me, that's not a plan.

Put your plan in writing. If you wince at the thought of approaching this holiday season with a written plan, afraid that it will turn spontaneity into rigidity, think about the alternative. Debt is the result of reacting impulsively. The more of Christmas you leave to chance, the greater the potential debt load you will carry into the next year.

Please don't resist the idea of making a plan, no matter how threatening or uncomfortable it may feel at first. Remember, don't trust your feelings. Once you and your family have decided what you want from the celebration of Christmas, you'll be able to make adjustments and corrections as the season unfolds and even treat yourselves to some deliciously spontaneous times along the way.

State your purpose. Your holiday plan should start with a purpose statement describing what you and your family want the holidays to look like. Simply write a sentence or two summarizing your ideal Christmas, making sure it reflects your family's values. There are no rules, no correct or incorrect responses. This is the way to tame the monster that used to come barreling in your life every December.

Use the calendar. Your holiday blueprint should be built around the calendar. It will assist you in managing your time and your holiday spending plan, which will help you manage your resources. Flip back to chapter 2 and review your responses to the queries about how you would have changed previous holidays. Let what you learned from the past guide you as you develop your plan for the Christmas ahead.

Plan according to your values. Consider holding a family meeting to create your family's "Top Five Holiday Values." Take nominations from each member of the family, and once you've decided on a final list, write it down and post it where everyone can see it.

Values may include enjoying the family, experiencing an old-fashioned simple Christmas, strengthening personal relationships, exchanging only gifts that cannot be purchased in stores, celebrating Christ's birth, eating glorious creations from the kitchen, attending musical performances, decorating the house, directing the school pageant, singing in the community choir, relaxing and resting, reaching out to those who are less fortunate, visiting relatives and entertaining friends, and so on.

Ask questions. In what specific ways can our values be expressed in our home and lives during the Christmas season? How can we share our blessings with other people?

If, for instance, one of your top five values is "Christmas is a time to spend more quality time together as a family," ask family members, "How specifically will we do that? And when?" If you decide that everyone will play hooky from work and school one day to do nothing but sleep in, play video games, put together a jigsaw puzzle, and bake Christmas cookies (which now that I think about it is the best idea I've had in a long time), then decide right now when that will be. Mark out the whole day on the calendar so nothing will interfere.

Or if one of your values is "Christmas is a time to exchange gifts with friends and family," answer specifically who, what, when, and how much. Wow! This is a lot of work, huh? Not really. Consider it a trade-off. Either you do the work now in a relaxed and reasoned way, or you'll have to do it the old way—on the fly and without much control.

Continue through your values list and watch as the calendar fills up. Keep in mind that many activities will come up to fill your holidays, activities that may not be included on your list. Address those issues now. Which activities will you decline? Which parties will you attend? What about the office parties and activities? Which days will you leave unscheduled to allow for free time? Which days will you devote to gift-making, shopping, and wrapping?

Include a holiday spending plan. It is vital that your holiday plan includes a specific and detailed spending plan, designating the overall amount you plan to spend and the ways you plan to spend it.

To start, make a chart that will allow you to visualize your spending categories, including gifts for kids, spouse, grandparents, other relatives, friends, service givers, co-workers, and employees; gift wrapping; Christmas cards, postage, and a photo session; baking ingredients; tree and home decorations; admission for holiday events; babysitting and travel costs; charitable donations; new clothes; etc.

In a column with the heading "Dollar Amount Plan," write down the amount of money you plan to spend on each category. Total all of the categories to see how much cash you will need for your expected holiday expenses. Whoa. It's probably a lot more dough than you anticipated or even have available at the moment.

Did you ever dream your holiday expenses were so huge? No wonder Christmas has sent you to the credit cards in the past.

I hope you've used a pencil because you'll probably need to do some (or a lot of) erasing and refiguring. First, erase the total and write instead the total cash amount you intend to have available to spend for the Christmas holidays. You may have to resharpen that pencil often before you get your expected spending to match your total available cash.

If the list is really out of balance—your expenses clearly exceed your available cash—start whittling down that enormous gift list. Many times we feel compelled to give a gift when a nice card, photo of the kids, or personal note would convey the intended goodwill. Go through your list with this in mind and put a star next to those who will be getting cards as gifts this year.

If you still have a discrepancy, there are two things you can do: reduce expenses even further or find ways to come up with more cash.

In the chapters that follow, I provide lots of ideas for low-cost and no-cost ways you can achieve your holiday expectations. A lack of cash should not eliminate your ability to give gifts.

Use the envelope system. Once you have a good spending plan in which your estimated expenses and available cash are on speaking terms, get a stack of envelopes and label one for each of your holiday-spending categories and for each person on your gift list. Place the amount of cash you intend to spend on each category and each person in the corresponding envelope and put the envelopes away in a safe place.

When you go holiday shopping, leave the credit cards at home and take the appropriate envelopes instead. It will be easy for you to keep track of expenses because you'll know precisely the moment you are finished spending—when the envelope is empty.

Enjoy the fringe benefits of cash spending. If you have been accustomed to paying for holiday shopping with credit cards, or even a checkbook, the all-cash method is going to feel very strange in the beginning. Expect to feel timid and fearful that you might run out of funds.

You may find yourself hesitant to spend "that much" of the available cash on a single gift. (Isn't it funny how a check, debit card, or credit card doesn't feel as real as actual cash?) Actually, these are helpful responses because they will make you think more carefully about your purchases. Spending cash will also compel you to find the best bargains.

When shopping with a limited amount of cash, you will be less prone to spend impulsively. You will become a disciplined consumer, and your entire holiday outlook will change.

One Christmas when I was twenty and my brother was seventeen, we were both out of work and worried about what we would be able to get our grandparents (who adopted us) for Christmas. My grandmother had been ill, and our family decided it would be too much trouble to pull out all the ornaments from the attic and get the tree up from the basement. For the first time in my life our house was not decorated.

One day my brother and I were taking a shortcut through the back parking lot of a row of stores when we saw, propped up against a trash dumpster, the prettiest Christmas tree just sitting there. We went inside the store and asked if the tree was going to be thrown away or if it belonged to someone who worked in the store. The manager asked the employees, and no one spoke up, so we asked the manager if we could take the tree. He said yes. I drove a VW Beetle at the time, and we had a hysterical time getting that tree home.

We silently set up the tree in the living room, and when we were finished, we wheeled our grandmother into the room and lit up the tree. The look on my grandmother's face was one of pure joy. I think she realized that my brother and I finally understood that Christmas had nothing to do with how many presents are under the tree.

Donna H., Texas

A tradition in our home is to limit our gift-giving to four specific categories. Each child receives a gift of love, which is something homemade; a gift of warmth, which is something like socks or a lap blanket; a gift of knowledge, such as a science kit, books, or educational DVD; and a gift of joy—that one thing they really want.

This has helped to keep our Christmas balanced, our budget small, and our gifts meaningful.

Nancy E., California

"I understand your predicament, Mr. Claus, and it's quite surprising to me that you even have a credit card, but I still need to see some ID."

4

Finding the Cash

You've made a commitment that you will not spend more money than you have. So no matter what the date, it's time to get prepared for a no-debt, paid-in-full Christmas. Ready?

Raise your right hand (or hands if you're doing this as a family, which would be such a great idea!) and repeat after me: I am [we are] fully committed not to incur debt to pay for any aspect of the Christmas holiday celebration. I [we] will not be guided by guilt or obligation and will do whatever it takes to keep all expenses well within the amount of money I [we] have to spend.

Place this written no-debt commitment in a prominent place in your home. The refrigerator door is a good place where the entire family will see it often. If you think of your goal in a positive and upbeat manner, your children will catch your enthusiasm and determination too.

You should be very proud of yourself. Perhaps for the first time you will be able to take the stress and dread out of the holidays. And even if you don't have time to implement every good idea in this book this year, you'll have a huge head start when you begin the New Year with a plan already in place for next Christmas.

Where's the Money?

Need to raise some cash quickly so you can avoid new debt this coming holiday season? No matter the date on the calendar, start crash saving right now. You'll be amazed at how much dough you can accumulate in a hurry.

Because you now have your holiday spending plan (or you will shortly—I have faith), you need to see that total amount as your savings goal.

Let's say you've determined that you will need twelve hundred dollars to cover all of your intended holiday expenses. If it is now January, you'll need to save one hundred dollars a month. That's an easy calculation. If, however, it's July, you'll need to step that up to two hundred dollars or more to meet your goal.

I think I hear you muttering that you can't do that. Really? Well, then you really can't spend twelve hundred dollars for Christmas or any amount over the amount of cash you will have saved by then. Perhaps you need to reduce your holiday expenses to six hundred dollars or an amount to match the number of months that remain if you are limited to a one-hundred-dollars-per-month rate of savings.

With your goal in place, it's a lot easier to start stashing cash. Just start thinking creatively. Here are a few ideas to help you jump-start your savings.

Pantry survival. More than likely you have enough food in your pantry, cupboards, and freezer to feed your family for at least a week or two. Skip the grocery store for a couple of weeks, eat what you already have, and stash the grocery money.

Eat in. If time is short, consider an extreme approach. No more fast food or restaurants between now and Christmas. Put the money you would have spent on fast food and eating out into your holiday stash.

Just water. If you do eat out, bribe yourself. When you order water only and skip the pricey beverages, slip two bucks into your stash.

Rethink a habit. We could all cut back or eliminate a few spending habits with little lasting impact on our lives. You don't have to eliminate the daily coffees, vending machine snacks, manicures, and pedicures altogether. Just think them through, make some cost-cutting adjustments, and consciously put the savings into your holiday stash on a regular basis. Do you really need to eat lunch out every day? Cut it back to two days, brown bag the other three, and stash the money you don't spend.

Coins and small bills. Every evening deposit the coins in your pocket or purse into a central collection spot. Ditto for the one-dollar bills and five-dollar bills. Make this a family affair and you'll accumulate cash even faster.

Expense account reimbursements. If you travel as part of your job or use your own funds in other ways for work, you probably get reimbursed by your company later. When you receive the reimbursement checks, don't even think about spending them. Instead, add the money to your holiday stash.

Coupons, refunds, and rebates. When you receive a refund or rebate for the purchase of a product at the supermarket or through the mail, don't spend it. Stash it in your special fund. At the grocery store, have all of your purchases subtotaled and write your check or swipe your debit card for this amount. Then have the checker reduce the total by your qualified coupons and receive those savings back in cash. Make sure you do not commingle the savings with your pocket cash. Then place the amount—no matter how small—into your stash.

Forgotten gift cards. Pool all family members' forgotten/neglected gift cards that are languishing in the bottom of drawers, purses, and wallets. Add them to the holiday stash.

My Christmas Club. There was a time when banks everywhere offered Christmas Club savings accounts for customers. A customer would fill out an authorization instructing the bank (or in some cases his or her employer) to automatically transfer a set amount from each paycheck to a savings account to be held specifically for Christmas shopping. Then at Thanksgiving a tidy sum of money would come in the mail—cash for Christmas. As little as ten dollars a week would result in a check for five hundred dollars. Just because most banks have long since discontinued their Christmas Club programs doesn't mean you can't create your own.

A little moonlight. Overtime, odd jobs, perhaps even a second job are all ways to create the cash you'll need for Christmas. Provided you are diligent to always stash those small additional incomes, you'll quickly accumulate the money you need to go all-cash.

Adjust tax withholding. This is delicate, so hear me out. If you routinely receive a refund when you file your income taxes, it means you are having too much money withheld from your paycheck. You are in essence giving the federal government an interest-free loan. You send in way too much money and tell them to keep what they need and send you a refund next year. That doesn't make much sense to me. If this is your situation, consider changing your withholding by filling out a new form with your employer and adjusting the number of exemptions you claim so that your withholding more closely resembles the amount of taxes you owe. But don't get used to the new amount. Arrange to automatically deposit the difference into your stash.

You'll be amazed how much cash you can accumulate in as little time as three or four weeks—money that might have otherwise leaked out of your life undetected. Determine to limit your holiday spending to just the cash you have and you'll give yourself an incredible gift: no new debt to follow you into the New Year!

More Cash-Saving Ideas

Here are more cash-saving ideas contributed by faithful fans and clever readers of the Debt-Proof Living newsletter:

 In order for everyone to be involved in saving for Christmas, we decorate a container with Christmas paper, glue the lid down, and make a slit in the top. At each person's pay period, he or she makes a set contribution and says a prayer for our debt-free holiday. Additional contributions can be made anytime during the year, with the only condition that a prayer must accompany the contribution. At Thanksgiving we break open the account and make our decisions on how we will spend the money. This is a great way to help children prioritize, and it gives meaning to a budget.

 Starting now, once a month put twenty dollars into an envelope for a service person you want to remember with a tip during the holidays. Label, seal, and don't forget where you put it.

Say no to credit come-ons. Don't even think about using those convenience checks often issued by banks and credit-card companies during the holiday season. Writing out one of those checks is equivalent to getting a cash advance, which may mean paying steep transaction fees and interest that is generally higher than that for purchases. Also, resist offers to skip a payment. It may sound like an unexpected gift from your bank or credit-card company, but don't be fooled. Interest will accumulate on your unpaid balance, so next month your balance will be even higher.

 Don't fall for the ploy to get 10 or 15 percent off when you apply for a store's credit card. Don't even think about that. The inquiry alone is not worth the potential one-time savings because your credit score will be negatively impacted. And you do not need the temptation of putting any holiday purchases on plastic.

 Use a small expandable folder (like you might use for supermarket coupons) to hold your holiday cash. Label each section with the names of your recipients. In each section, keep a list of ideas for that person, the cash you plan to spend on them, and receipts once the items are purchased. If a gift needs to be returned, you'll know exactly where the receipt is. You can use this "wallet" year-round to purchase birthday or other holiday gifts, to collect ideas for next Christmas, and to keep you on the debt-proof track.

 Here is a painless way to accumulate cash for the holidays. Start each month with a zero balance in your checkbook (don't carry over your balance from last month). Don't pay attention to how much you're "forgetting." You won't believe how quickly it adds up!

 To raise cash for holiday shopping, we play "The Pantry Game" in our house. We pretend we're stranded on a desert island and the only nourishment we have is what is presently in the pantry, refrigerator, and freezer. There's no way we will be rescued for a week. It becomes a challenge to create meals from our precious resources. Our motivation? The grocery money that week goes into the holiday stash. We went for a full two weeks one time, buying only milk during our "ordeal."

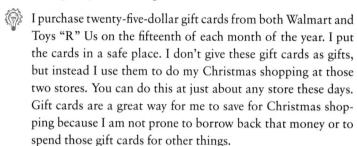 I purchase twenty-five-dollar gift cards from both Walmart and Toys "R" Us on the fifteenth of each month of the year. I put the cards in a safe place. I don't give these gift cards as gifts, but instead I use them to do my Christmas shopping at those two stores. You can do this at just about any store these days. Gift cards are a great way for me to save for Christmas shopping because I am not prone to borrow back that money or to spend those gift cards for other things.

Place a festively decorated jar in a prominent place in your house to remind you to collect spare change for those in need.

It was the Christmas of 1998, and my mother was very ill and unable to go out and shop for Christmas. She hadn't been out of the house for anything other than doctor visits for the previous several years. Nonetheless, on Christmas morning under the Christmas tree there was a plain white envelope with "Johnny" scrawled on it in her handwriting. In the envelope was an old, crumpled ten-dollar bill.

Thinking back on that now, I realize that that ten-dollar bill was the most wonderful gift I had ever received as a Christmas present. That old bill must have been stuffed back in her purse for years—"saved for a rainy day," as she would have put it. Apparently, she was aware that her "rainy day" had come, because that was her last Christmas with us. This memory has been my own private Christmas joy for the years since she died.

John W., Texas

At my church, we raise money for our annual Easter party by holding a pre-Christmas children's flea market. We ask the children and parents of our congregation to consider donating some of their like-new, unused, or unopened toys to our flea market. We emphasize that the children should be the ones to decide which toys they will give, with the help of their parents. We collect the toys over two weeks, arrange them on tables by age group or category, and hold a big flea market in the beginning of December, in time for the Christmas rush.

We think it is a win-win situation for everyone concerned. Kids in our church learn to give, parents get to declutter the house and make room for the inevitable new toys, anyone looking for a deal gets a great bargain, and the church gets help funding the Easter party!

Andrea H., New Jersey

5

Getting a Holiday Head Start

If you are or ever have been plagued by consumer debt, I can nearly guarantee that revolving expenses related to Christmas have contributed greatly to that miserable situation.

The problem? Procrastination. Face it, when it comes to Christmas, the longer you wait, the more you'll spend. The opposite is also true. The sooner you get started, the less you'll spend.

Everyone procrastinates in some area. And some people procrastinate about everything. Why do we do it?

We feel overwhelmed. The holiday expectations we place on ourselves, plus those that come from our families, the community, and even the church, can be so great that we feel paralyzed. So we do nothing until the only choice we think we have is to spend as much money as it takes to get by.

We overestimate how much time we need. The task appears to be so overwhelming that we assume it will take forever. So rather than doing even a little bit, we do nothing.

We overestimate how much time we have. From where we sit during the year, Christmas seems so far away. We tell ourselves we have plenty of time.

We overestimate our abilities. If we believe we can finish a task in three hours, we put it off until only three hours remain. That leaves no margin, no room for error—no allowance for the law of life that says things rarely go as planned.

We have to do it perfectly. Experts tell us that at the root of procrastination is perfectionism. Because we feel we have to do everything perfectly—and fear we may not—we do nothing rather than run the risk of failing.

We say we work better under pressure. Waiting until the last minute can provide quite an adrenaline rush. We believe we cannot operate without that creative surge, and so we sit back and wait for it to happen.

The way to deal with procrastination is to identify why you do it. As it relates specifically to the topic of Christmas, ask yourself:

What price have I paid in the past for the delay?

Do I really want to pay that price, or even more, again this year?

If the answer to the last question is yes, drop everything and get to the beach. You have lots of time; you don't need to be thinking about the holidays yet.

If, on the other hand, you are not willing to go into debt, there are simple things you can do to stop procrastinating.

Get started. Do something to get moving. Once you are in motion, it will be easier to keep going.

Write it down. Reduce your plans to paper. Seeing things in black and white eliminates the unknown and provides a realistic playing field. Set reasonable limits both in time and in money.

Work with the time you have. Make a simple time line, then break the project down into small, manageable parts. Even five minutes is enough time to get something done when you have a plan.

Set a series of small deadlines. As an example, give yourself a date one week from today to have your gift list written. Share your deadlines with someone who will keep you accountable.

Find the simpler way. To minimize the powerful emotions of the season, determine ways you can reasonably scale back and simplify. Make room in your holiday plans for relaxation and enjoyment.

Be opportunistic. Whether it's picking up shells along the shore to adorn a picture frame or finding a bargain collectible at a tag sale during your summer vacation, over the next few months or weeks many opportunities will present themselves, so take full advantage.

Plan now. The problem for most of us comes down to a combination of not planning and not thinking about the financial impact of holiday spending. It's easier not to. It's just too overwhelming. Besides, who can get into a holiday mood in the heat of summer?

Have you ever thought that the very reason you don't want to think about Christmas now may be the best reason you should? While you are not involved emotionally is the time you can think the most rationally. You're not dealing with holiday sights and sounds that render you defenseless. That makes this the best time to get a grip on this year's holiday spending.

Be realistic. A big part of the problem is that the December holidays aren't just about gifts. There are decorations, holiday clothes, parties and trips, special concerts and plays, postage for cards and parcels, and, of course, all that food. The obvious solution is not to spend a lot of money on any of these things. Think about alternative ways to make the holidays happy.

Shop early. One way to trim holiday expenses is to start gift shopping early and to make use of sales and specials throughout the year. Perhaps you can buy one or two gifts a month starting now. Just make sure you keep track of what you've purchased, for whom you have purchased it, and where it's hidden.

Stay alert. There are many things you can do throughout the year that will require very little time and little, if any, money, but these tiny efforts will multiply come Christmas.

Combine holidays. Think about how many holidays share the colors and symbols that can be incorporated into Christmas. Valentine's Day offers hearts of every size and material, red candies, red paper goods and wrapping paper, and red and white candles. St. Patrick's Day brings an array of everything in the color green: green candles, green paper goods, green ribbon and papers. Easter brings out loads of baskets and big plastic eggs that can be used for unusual and unique gift presentations. Thanksgiving is the time to pick up gourds, small pumpkins, and other cheap accessories that can be painted and included in wreaths, garlands, and gift wrapping. Make sure you're thinking Christmas as you check out those day-after-the-holiday, near-giveaway prices.

Shop on vacations. What better time to pick up all kinds of things you'll be able to use at Christmas than when you're away from your usual surroundings? Seashells make wonderful additions to packages, wreaths, and garlands. Museum gift shops often offer low-cost and unusual items that will make wonderful gifts and decorations. You're not under pressure here; just keep your eyes open and your brain in gear.

Visit thrift shops and flea markets. As you visit these shops and events during the year, watch out for small pieces of antique lace, doilies, buttons, buckles, and so on. Use them to make a gorgeous Victorian tree, wreath, or garland. Framed pages from old children's books can be a wonderful gift for a new baby's nursery.

Reuse old toys. Anything vintage of the toy or stuffed animal nature can make wonderful nostalgic displays in your home at Christmastime.

Collect miscellaneous items. There are many things you can collect during the year in order to take the pressure off the month of December. Mason jars, unusual glass containers, and narrow-necked bottles can hold gifts from the kitchen; brown grocery bags or shopping bags can be used to wrap gifts; white bakery bags and candles can be used to make luminaries; mailing tubes and paper towel rolls make unusual gift wrapping or party favors; the tops from frozen juice containers can be turned into ornaments; and corks can be used to make stamps.

Explore the craft market. Hundreds of books and websites offer craft ideas—from the simplest to the most complex and everything in between. Check out the possibilities at your local library. The following chapters also offer ideas. You'll find dozens of unique uses for dried roses, pieces of cardboard, old corks, and seashells.

Trust yourself. Let's say it looks like you'll have a bumper crop of berries this summer. You decide to make lots of your signature freezer jam, which will be the inspiration for holiday gift baskets in December. Great idea! Find a recipe for biscuits, which will be the perfect basket companion along with other items you can start accumulating now.

A note of caution for you: Come Christmas, as you are putting your baskets together, a little voice may start whispering in your ear. It will suggest your gifts aren't good enough, you need to go buy some real gifts, and your biscuits and jam theme is silly. You know it's going to happen, so plan on it. Then determine that you will not listen, choosing rather to trust yourself and to believe in your plan.

Any time of the year is the best time of the year to start thinking about the most wonderful time of the year. The pressure is off, so you can think clearly. And a stress-free Christmas is likely the very best gift you can give yourself and your family.

We started a tradition thirty years ago, and it has become a gift no money can buy. As my husband put away the Christmas decorations on a cold, dreary January afternoon, he tucked a little note in the box that described a few of the events that had happened that Christmas: the weather, the people who stopped in for a visit, and a few words about our hopes, dreams, and wishes for the New Year. The next year it was so much fun to discover that little note tucked in with our Christmas things.

That was the year we started the memories box. Every Christmas holiday we make sure we write a note reflecting on the past year and some of the events that happened in our lives. Often we add a few resolutions or hopes for the upcoming year. We ask family members who are with us for the holidays to join in on this tradition.

As children came into our lives, we eventually had them write little notes as well. Some years I have made up a page with questions to make the task easier. We place these notes into a special wooden box and keep it closed until the next year on Christmas Eve, when we take them out and read them together.

It is always amazing to refresh a good memory and hear how things have changed and dreams have come true. After thirty years, we have a true gift of memories stored up in our wooden box. We have notes from loved ones who are no longer with us; scribbled notes from when our children were young; thoughtful notes from when they got older and appreciated things differently; notes reflecting on happy memories, special trips, decisions needing to be made, broken hearts that mended, favorite foods, favorite movies, and many aspirations.

Karen H., Missouri

6

Holiday Dilemmas

The results are in and the news is shocking. According to the National Retail Federation, the average spending per person for Christmas 2010 was $719.[1] The most popular gifts were clothing, books, CDs, DVDs, videos or video games, toys, home-decor-related items, and jewelry.

And how did we pay for all that loot? Americans added more than $2.3 billion to their credit-card debt in December 2010 alone![2] God only knows how much of that staggering increase remained unpaid six months later.

I know a thing or two about extreme holiday spending. For years I did my part to keep up with national averages. And it nearly killed me. Extreme comes quite easily for many of us in these days when credit is so available. Merchants are foaming at the mouth for us to accept creative billing, new lines of credit, promises of zero interest, or no payments until years from now.

But what if we decided to take Christmas to the other extreme? We could take our cues from those who've bucked the trend—and found unexpected joy as a result.

In the tiny tome *Hundred Dollar Holiday,* author Bill McKibben offers a simple and inviting strategy for handling the most complicated holiday of the year—Christmas. He argues in favor of spending only one hundred dollars. "The Christmas we now celebrate grew up at a time when Americans were mostly poor . . . mostly working with their hands and backs," he writes. "If we now feel burdened and unsatisfied by the piles of gifts and over-consuming, it is not because Christmas has changed all that much." He adds, "It's because we have."[3]

One reader wrote about her best Christmas ever—the year when her father lost his job. Rather than grouse about being poor and pitiful, he declared that everyone in the family would still exchange gifts. The catch? They could spend no money at all. Christmas morning was more magical than any she can recall before or after. Her prize gift was from her father: a wristwatch he found in the trash, lovingly disassembled, cleaned, repaired, and polished to a more glorious condition than new.

Another family made the bold move that among their rather large extended family gifts could not be purchased new. That still left many options for holiday shopping, albeit off the beaten path: garage sales, thrift stores, even the givers' own attics and basements. Everyone spent far less but became far more engaged by pouring their hearts and souls into finding a uniquely perfect gift.

Over and over again the stories I receive from people who choose to give gifts in a manner contrary to what our highly commercialized society would have preferred reveal some kind of magic. Choosing to go against the tide of extreme shopping, they find a new kind of joy. They learn things that they never knew before about the people they love. Hidden talents rise to the surface; creativity is ignited. Excitement and anticipation are reborn and pressure relieved.

Just think. If you have the courage to lift the financial burden from the next holiday season by setting new extreme ground rules, you won't create new debt and you won't rip through your savings to buy gifts for people who probably won't even remember what you gave them come January. But most of all, for perhaps the first time ever, you will really enjoy the season, knowing that you've made an extreme move to change it up—to do everything differently.

Gift-Giving Dilemmas

There is no way I could possibly list all of the various family situations and dynamics that come into play around the holidays. But allow me to mention a few. If your particular situation is not mentioned, go ahead and add it in as we wade into this matter. I'm sure it is just a variation on a more general theme.

Usually, family angst springs out of the matter of gift-giving. And the larger the family, the more conflict likely to arise—conflict that is nearly always tied to money. Here are a few typical scenarios.

Limiters versus balkers. Large families usually have at least one member who tries to convince everyone to limit gift-giving in some way so as to relieve the financial pressure of exchanging individual gifts. And without fail, there will be at least one member who balks. The balker thinks the one suggesting a way to cut back is cheap and selfish. The limiter is just sure the balker is in debt up to her eyeballs and that she wants everyone else to join her. The limiter sees the balker as wanting to impress everyone with her limitless wealth, while the balker feels ripped off and dissatisfied because she's the only one who really cares enough to give spectacular gifts. This situation creates hard feelings, resentment, and dread.

Singles or childless couples versus large families. Oh, this is a touchy one! This scenario involves a rather large family with lots of cousins and grandchildren. Invariably, there will be at least one single adult and/ or a couple with no children. The family with eight children sees no problem giving the single person or childless couple one gift from the entire family but fully expects individual gifts for all their kids. If you've experienced this, you know what I'm talking about. If not, just imagine.

The financially challenged versus big spenders. In this difficult situation, someone in the family circle is quite well-to-do and also generous with the wealth. Read: great gifts! And that makes the financially challenged family nervous. They don't know how to respond except to assume they need to exchange gifts in the same price range. When they are unable to do that—or they go into debt in order to keep up—it can create all kinds of negative feelings.

Okay, so how close did I come to hitting on your personal situation? Of course, there are variations on these themes. I've heard of families in which the parents are wealthy and all the adult children are starting out on their own without the financial resources to pony up gifts worthy of the parents' approval. Or maybe the kids are lavish with the gifts but the parents are unable to respond in kind. Whatever the arrangement or division of resources within an extended family—as uneven as it may be—a lot of energy is wasted trying to get this gift-giving thing just right.

New Ways to Give

What we need are ways to deal with these kinds of unreasonable expectations, guilt, and hurt feelings. And the solution begins with courage—courage to give as you want to give, not out of guilt or expectation; courage to spend what you can on what you desire, not what others say you must.

You need courage to get creative, to try something new, and to be patient while others get on board with your brilliant ideas. Easier said than done? Perhaps. But give things a chance. I think you will be amused if not pleasantly surprised to learn what others have done and with great results. If not, at least you will be entertained. And you'll have plenty to talk about.

We have a tradition in our home that has been going on for more than thirty years. When our boys were only toddlers, we and our best friends, who have three children just about the same ages as our boys, decided that we would have a family Christmas party early in December. We called it a family party even though the two families are not technically related. We invited two sets of grandparents and one other older couple as well. Our common bond? Five adorable kids and all the grown-ups who love them. Everyone dressed up, and the children performed their current talent. We had such a great time that we decided to make this family Christmas party an annual event.

That first year there were a few gifts—mostly small things for the children. But somehow over the years, the gifts grew in both quantity and quality. Last Christmas this event passed the thirty-five-year mark. Four of the five babies are now married with babies of their own. Lots of kids! Four grandparents have died, so the family dynamic has changed tremendously. But still the family Christmas party goes on. And every year the problem arises: what to do about gifts?

I give you this background so you can fully appreciate what happened a couple of years ago. The host (we switch hosting every year) mailed instructions for how the adults would exchange gifts (everyone would still bring gifts for the children). She put all the names of the adults into a hat and drew one for each. The instructions stated that we were to shop and "buy" for that person what we would if we had all the money in the world. How? Find a picture or other visual representation of the object. The instructions explained that we should come to the party with our gift properly wrapped and be prepared to give the reasons we chose it.

The day the instructions arrived in the mail, I got a call from my mother-in-law, Gwen. She was livid! "What on earth is this all about?" she queried. "Has Kathleen lost her mind?" For days Gwen was agitated and quite upset. She was happy with the person's name she drew but not at all happy about this ridiculous non-gift way of giving a gift. I tried to help her think outside the box of typical Christmas gifting. But she was not at all enthusiastic.

There were a few other grumblers, but mostly everyone was willing to try. I did notice a lack of enthusiasm, especially in my immediate family, and I was slightly apprehensive too.

The night of the party there was an air of cautious anticipation, but no one was more visibly excited than my mother-in-law. I figured she'd done what she'd threatened to do: bring a store-bought gift in defiance of this ridiculous idea.

As people opened their gifts, the fun began. One flying enthusiast got a new jet. Wow, it was a beaut. It came as a framed picture complete with a list of amenities. Others received beautiful new homes, luxury automobiles, a complete domestic staff, diamonds, golf courses—the sky was truly the limit! And then Wendy opened her gift from Grandma (my mother-in-law). I tried not to look for fear it was not at all in keeping with the night's theme. But to my surprise, Gwen had spent days preparing a small scrapbook filled with beautiful pictures she'd found in magazines and catalogs, carefully picked out just for Wendy.

It was a moment to remember as Grandma so proudly gave Wendy all the things she knew she would love.

Not only was that the best gift exchange ever, but I also learned something important. Buying a gift is too easy. Creating a gift—even if it is cut from the pages of a magazine—requires the giver to think about the recipient and open his or her heart to that person.

What a memorable gift exchange we had. No one overspent, no one went into debt, no one went home with yet another dust catcher. There was no guilt, no unmet expectations. It was a sweet and carefree time to share the best gifts we could think of—things that would please and delight others. And no one enjoyed it more than my mother-in-law, whom we all agreed was the best gift-giver of all.

Don't wait. Start planning now. Contact your family members to see what creative ideas they can contribute. Don't worry. I have a feeling they are going to love your suggestions for how next Christmas you can spend less to enjoy more.

I don't profess to have the answer to every family's gift-giving situation. But I can share general guidelines, principles, and ideas from other families who have solved their situation, replacing gift-exchange strife with satisfying joy.

Members of Debt-Proof Living online offer these great ideas for big groups:

 If your family, office, or other group draws names at Christmas, think about changing that to drawing wish lists. Now, instead of receiving dust collectors or gag gifts to be enjoyed for a moment, everyone stands the chance of getting a gift they really want and will enjoy. Here's how it works. Early in the year (like at Thanksgiving when you are together), each person in the group fills out a questionnaire answering questions like these: What is your favorite color, fragrance, musician, actor, sports figure, sweet treat, author, toy, hobby, pastime, magazine? What do you collect? What's missing from your collection? What would you do with an extra twenty bucks? Make sure each person's name is on his or her wish list. Fold them up and drop them into a hat. Now, instead of drawing names, draw lists. Use the list of personal preferences when selecting a gift for the person whose name you've been assigned. Dollar limit? Sure, if you want; it's optional.

Our family is hardly ever together for Christmas and often not at all during the year either. We came up with an alternative to drawing names. We established a permanent rotation of sibling names so we know who we'll be buying gifts for a year in advance.

Here's a great idea for a Secret Santa gift exchange. Choose a recipe for a treat, then give the recipient one ingredient at a time, placed in small zip-type bags. You can spread the gift over several days, even a week. For the last day, prepare the recipe and present it to your pal with the recipe attached to duplicate at home with all the ingredients received in the previous days.

Since several of our family members live out of state, I developed a questionnaire I send to each person every year. This updates sizes, colors, wants, and needs. I carry the information in my purse at all times.

If there is someone on your list with whom you would like to stop exchanging gifts at the holidays, send that person a note in early fall saying that you're cutting back and won't be sending gifts this year. Or just bring it up the next time you see him or her. The key is to let everyone know well in advance. They will probably be relieved not to buy you one too!

Our extended family now numbers thirty-two. By unanimous consent, we have agreed that gifts will be limited to the kids age twelve and under. We send the money the adults would have spent on gifts for one another to an inner-city school for abandoned and abused kids that is struggling to keep its doors open.

Hate the office gift exchange? This year suggest something new. Instead of buying a grown-up gift, buy a toy you believe your recipient would have loved as a child. Think long and hard. You'll be amazed at just how creative people can be. And when the party's over, put all the toys back into their boxes and deliver them to a charity or a Toys for Tots collection bin.

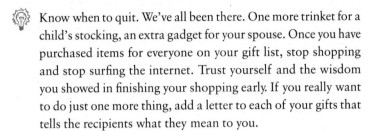 Know when to quit. We've all been there. One more trinket for a child's stocking, an extra gadget for your spouse. Once you have purchased items for everyone on your gift list, stop shopping and stop surfing the internet. Trust yourself and the wisdom you showed in finishing your shopping early. If you really want to do just one more thing, add a letter to each of your gifts that tells the recipients what they mean to you.

Because I refuse to go broke for Christmas gifts, I have told family members I am giving presents they can use and I can afford. My tip is if your relatives admire something of yours and you can part with it, give it to them! You already know they will like it, and you'll reduce clutter in your house at the same time.

In recent years on Christmas Eve, I have followed the tradition of reading aloud to my family from Laura Ingalls Wilder's Little House on the Prairie. For me, it is a great story of the spirit of giving, the importance of family, and the joy that comes from simple gifts (a new tin cup, a stick of candy, a cake made of white flour and white sugar, and a shiny, new penny). In this fast-paced, commercialized world, I revel in a few peaceful moments to reflect on this valuable story.

A few years ago, I gave each family member the above-mentioned items. They understood the deep meaning behind the gifts, and they use their cups and look at their pennies each Christmas.

Now that I have started my own family, I intend to continue this tradition with my children so that they too can be reminded of what Christmas is all about.

Nicole B., Ontario, Canada

"First, I'd like to know just exactly how you intend to finance this great giveaway!"

7

The Gentle Art
of Gift-Giving

The simple act of gift-giving has become extremely complicated. I blame that on the consumer-credit industry. Think about it. You can be completely broke but still spend thousands of dollars on Christmas gifts—and believe it is not only your right to do so but also your obligation to do so. We believe the message that we have to spend a lot for Christmas gifts to be socially acceptable.

Gift-giving is a custom that has pretty much run amok. But it doesn't have to be that way. We can choose to make wise and reasonable decisions about the gifts we give.

How many of you cannot recall the gifts you gave last Christmas? How about the gifts you received? Come on, let's see those hands. Okay, that's just about everybody.

It's not because we're total ingrates that we have trouble remembering the gifts we received. It's because when it's all over, the gifts pale in comparison to the joy they deliver—the love and best wishes for the season. That's what we carry with us from one year to the next.

Gifts are messengers. They are tokens of the esteem we hold for people we care about. They deliver our love and our best wishes. Gifts express the fondness we have for another person. Without the care, love, or concern, the gift is empty. Giving a gift just so you can mark a name off a list is a hollow effort that is likely to fall flat no matter how much money you spend.

Okay, so here's another question. How many of you still have a sense of the joy and good feelings associated with gift-giving that took place in your home and your life last Christmas, even if you cannot recall the specific gifts? Look at that. Hands are going up all over the room! At least some of those gifts did their job. They delivered joy and love and then quietly slipped out of the spotlight.

Those of you who couldn't raise your hands may be remembering the stress of finding the perfect gift, the hassle because you waited until the last minute. You may be recalling your guilt over spending money you didn't have on things you don't remember and haven't yet paid for.

If you struggle with the thought that gifts you give must fulfill the recipients' deepest longings and fondest dreams, think of the gifts you will give in the same way you would think of a special meal you prepare. You want it to be delicious and for your guests to enjoy it thoroughly. But no matter how fluffy your mashed potatoes or delectable the prime rib, your guests will stop eating and the meal will end. That doesn't mean it wasn't delicious and they didn't enjoy it. They will take away the memories of the flavors and the joy with which the meal was prepared and served. In that same way, your gifts should bring a momentary sense of joy, but it's the memories of your expression that will live on.

If you don't know what to give someone, ask this simple question: What matters to him or her? You have to know this person pretty well to know the answer to that question without inquiring. You almost have to be a detective. You have to pay attention, listen, and observe.

Let's say your grandmother really loves animals. In fact, she volunteers at the shelter two days a week. She is passionate about animal rights. Donating twenty dollars in her name to the animal shelter would probably make her break down and cry. She would be touched that you cared enough to figure out what really matters to her.

Not every occasion requires a gift. Sometimes a card that you buy or make yourself in which you write a thoughtful sentiment is an excellent way to go. Caring enough to pick out the right card and then taking the time and effort to write in it can say "I care!" even better than a gift could.

Being a responsible gift-giver will help you to be an excellent recipient as well. Knowing that it's the thought that went into the gift that counts—not the price tag—will help you to be genuinely grateful. You cannot be too grateful. But you can fail to express your gratitude, and that's always a bad thing.

Consider these idea starters:

Give something you made. Whether it's something from your kitchen, craft room, woodworking shop, or computer, there's nothing like a homemade gift. A tree ornament, plate of cookies, box of fudge, note cards—these are just some of the homemade gifts with universal appeal.

Give the gift of compassion. Do you want your gift to say how much you care? Then find a way to show you care about what matters most to that person. Is he or she passionate about medical research? Become a bone marrow donor. An environmentalist? Donate to an organization that reforests, and plant a tree in his or her name. Find something this person will find meaningful and then do it in his or her honor. Write a description of your experience and give it to your recipient.

Give what you do best. Often the most meaningful gifts and the most difficult ones to give are those that cost no money at all. A gift from the heart is a gift of time and talent. What do you do well? Cook, clean, babysit, garden, sew, drive, shop? Whatever it is, create a unique gift certificate and make what you do the gift that you give: a weekend of babysitting, a day of housecleaning, six hours of errand running. Follow up within just a few days to set the exact time your certificate will be redeemed. Your recipient may be too embarrassed to remind you to make good on the gift.

Give it in writing. Worried that your gifts—homemade or otherwise—are too cheap or not exactly right? All of your doubts will vanish when you include a short note with the gifts telling the recipients what they mean to you and the value they bring to your life.

The best gift is one that delivers a message of love and joy that remains with the recipient long after the gift has been consumed, used, or put away.

Tipping Points

It is a social custom to give cash gifts (tips, gratuities) at the holiday season. How this custom came to be I have no idea. Thankfully, there are no rules and no tipping police.

Sure, you will see a plethora of tipping guidelines in newspapers and magazines during the holidays, but they are editorial suggestions. Some I've read are mind-boggling and include the garbage man, newspaper delivery person, mail carrier, nanny, driver, and doorman; the housekeeper, butler, and maid (oh sure, don't we all have one of those?), which begs the question: What makes one service person worthy of gratuities from his or her patrons, while others—like grocery checkers—are not included?

Gratuities or tips, if you plan to give any, need to be part of your holiday spending plan, and that means you need to start thinking about them right now. If you're not sure, ask yourself, "Can I afford to be without this person?" And I do not mean afford as in a monetary sense. By "afford to be without" I mean do you want to face the future without this person's services? If you absolutely cannot bear the thought, then a tip is likely in order as an expression of gratitude for the service provided throughout the year and the fact that you do depend on him or her.

Before we even get to dollar amounts, general guidelines suggest that you look to a number of factors such as quality of service, frequency of service, how long you've used the service, customs in your area, and your personal financial situation.

There are no laws or even social standards when it comes to tipping. As you determine what is right for you, keep in mind that you have already paid these people for services rendered. Ask yourself, "Am I particularly grateful because this person made my life easier or did more than required?" For those who rate a yes, express your gratitude in a way that fits your ability, not according to what you think is expected.

Following are a few commonly accepted guidelines for your thoughtful consideration; however, keep in mind that social custom varies from one area to another. Also, set your own guidelines that fit within your means and the desires of your heart.

The garbage man. For me, the foregoing qualifiers eliminate the garbage man. I wouldn't have a clue who he is, to be honest. Some big robotic truck comes down our street and plucks the containers with a big mechanical arm and dumps them. So if that guy quits his driving job, I'm sure there are plenty of others willing to step up. His service is appreciated, but he personally is not essential in my life. No tip. If you actually know the person who collects your trash, a tip of fifteen to twenty dollars is customary.

The hairdresser. My hairdresser is a slightly different story. It does take a while to get in sync, and after a couple of years, I'm about there with this one. If you are happy with the service—even if your hairdresser is the owner of the salon—give 15 to 20 percent of the total bill on a typical visit (in addition to the tip you would normally leave for your last visit before the holidays) and a small gift. If you aren't happy, find a new hairdresser.

The yard guy. Yes, I have a landscape maintenance company that services our property. Being out of debt does have its luxuries. They do fine, but believe me, if they go out of business, I have my pick of about fifty others that will do the same thing. No tip.

The ant guy. We must live on the mother of all anthills. We have had ant problems since we bought this house twenty-five years ago. The ant guy comes routinely to spray and bait for ants. The company we use now is courteous and responsive, but so are other pest control services. I use this one because their price is about half of all the others and the service is adequate. No tip.

The housekeeper. This is a luxury that has become a total necessity in my life. I find that my sanity is worth paying someone to clean my house once a month. She is an angel. A gift from on high. She is punctual, immaculate, trustworthy, and reliable. She has a key to my house. I would trust her with my champion purebred dog (I don't have one, but if I did . . .). If she were to leave me, I would be devastated. I could not replace her in a million years. I give her raises when she least expects them. It is the best money I spend in any given month. I pray for her health, that she will live long and prosper. I want to be her favorite client so if a doctor somewhere ever says she can clean only one house, it will be mine! I give her a huge tip. Gladly. If you are happy with the service, the equivalent of up to one visit is appropriate.

The postal carrier. The US Postal Service forbids carriers from accepting cash; however, they may accept a nominal item with a value under twenty dollars, like cookies or chocolate, for example. If you are very pleased with your service, a letter of appreciation to the supervisor would be in order.

The babysitter. For a regular sitter on whom you depend and who consistently gives excellent care, Tipping.org suggests a tip equal to two nights' pay and a small gift from the children.

The newspaper delivery person. If you have daily delivery and you know who your delivery person is, fifteen to twenty-five dollars is appropriate. If that person delivers on the weekend only, give five to fifteen dollars.

The door personnel. If you live in a building with a doorman, a twenty-five- to one-hundred-dollar tip is typical, more or less depending on how much this person assists you during the year.

The superintendent. If your building has a "super" on whom you depend, a tip is highly recommended—particularly if you are fond of heat in the winter and air conditioning in the summer.

A monetary gift in any amount is one way to say thanks to service providers, but it is not the only way. Never underestimate the value of a handwritten note on pretty holiday stationery. A gift of homemade cookies or other special treats with a nice note is always appropriate and appreciated. Any expression of gratitude that comes from your heart is never wrong.

Charitable Giving

Tax-exempt organizations are the fastest-growing sector in the US economy. In 2010, American donors contributed almost $291 billion to charitable causes, according to Giving USA, a report compiled annually by the American Association of Fundraising Counsel.[4] There are now 1.6 million nonprofit organizations, and the competition for funds has become intense.

Giving away part of what we earn is one of the pillars of debt-proof living. We give as an expression of gratitude and to teach our brains that, all things considered, we really do have more than enough. Giving quiets insatiable desires, takes the focus off ourselves, and pulls the plug on greed.

A recent study[5] reveals that knowing our money is going to a good cause activates the pleasure centers of our brains, giving us a sense of joy. We feel better when we make a voluntary donation. Here are some guidelines to follow when giving to charity.

Know your charity. The only way to avoid getting ripped off is to have knowledge of the charity you support. As a donor, you should know what they do with the money that is donated to them and how they accomplish their charitable mission. Give to charities whose work you can observe in your own community. You can request written literature and a copy of the charity's latest annual report. This should include a list of the board of directors, a mission statement, and the most recent available audited financial statement with accompanying notes. The most reputable charities spend no more for administrative costs than twenty-five cents from each dollar donated.

Beware of charities bearing gifts and sob stories. The hard-luck appeal is a favorite of some organizations. But someone has to pay for all those greeting cards, address labels, and other "free gifts." And you can be sure it's the donations of those who've come before you. Be suspicious of phone solicitors or direct mail appeals that tell you nothing of the charity or offer vague explanations of where the charity is headquartered, who runs the organization, and how they intend to spend your charitable dollars.

Keep records of your donations. Do not give cash and do not give your credit-card number to a telephone solicitor. Give your gift by check or money order so you will have a record for tax purposes. The IRS requires that you obtain a receipt from the charity (a canceled check will not suffice) for all tax-deductible contributions.

When you donate non-cash items of clothing, household goods, books, magazines, computer equipment, and automobiles, make sure you keep good records. You will receive a receipt describing your donation, but the IRS requires you, the donor, to determine the fair market value of the items you donate. Most people don't have a clue what their things are worth, so they estimate too low. Look for free online valuation guidelines at SalvationArmyUSA.org.

Remember that "tax exempt" does not always mean "tax deductible." Not all charities soliciting for "good causes" are eligible to receive tax-deductible contributions. "Tax exempt" means the organization does not have to pay taxes. "Tax deductible" means the donor (that's you) can deduct contributions on his or her federal income tax return. Request the charity's tax-exempt letter indicating its status with the IRS if you have any doubts.

Use resources. Both the Better Business Bureau (www.bbb.org) and the American Institute of Philanthropy (www.charitywatch.org) operate as watchdogs over charities. They offer excellent information to help you become a wise donor.

Exercise wisdom. Gift-giving is both a privilege and a responsibility. If you can see yourself as a steward or manager of resources that have been trusted to your care, you will look at this matter through new eyes.

Members of Debt-Proof Living online offer these gift-giving tips:

 In our city, the larger department stores have charity drives. They give gift cards to people who bring in gently used items for charity. I take the opportunity to declutter my home and then use the cards for gifts. That's a deal where everyone wins.

 Put the brakes on gift-giving. The truth is that parents are more concerned with multiple, lavish gifts than are most children. And the overload of more presents than a child can cope with doesn't increase his joy, just his greediness. Why not involve the children in giving to a local shelter or bringing canned and packaged food to a food bank? Family activities such as these can help remind children of how much they have and keep the focus on the real meaning of Christmas.

 Pare down. If your children already have lots of toys (tell me, what kids don't?), here is a way you can help them become givers and at the same time make room for what will come on Christmas. Help them go through all their toys and designate those that are still in good shape but no longer played with. Clean them up and make sure they are in good working order. Donate them to a shelter or orphanage that accepts gently used toys, games, and stuffed animals. Take the kids with you when you make the delivery so they understand there is a world beyond them with children who are less fortunate.

Make a contribution to a charity in the name of your recipient. The organization will send an acknowledgment card announcing your generosity. Any dollar amount is appreciated, and the exact amount of your donation is not typically disclosed.

Join the Big Brothers or Big Sisters program in your area. You'll be making a Christmas gift of yourself to a youngster in need of adult direction and inspiration.

Adult children often have trouble knowing what to give their parents because many parents don't really need anything. Last year our kids took the test to become potential bone marrow donors. The previous year they all donated blood to the Red Cross as their gift to us.

Last year I introduced the idea of alternative gift-giving to the adults on my Christmas list. For family members, I made simple ornaments and then donated to a charity related to each one's special interest. For my brother, the avid baseball fan, I donated to a charity for low-income kids' recreation. For my co-workers, I made layered soup in a jar and included a note telling them that I had made a donation to a local soup kitchen in their honor.

After spending too much money on gifts that were the wrong size, wrong style, and wrong idea, I decided that this year I would plant trees in honor of the people on my list. I contacted a local environmental group and volunteered to participate in a reforestation project. I worked hard but spent no money. I made up a beautiful certificate for each person and included it in their

Christmas card. Everyone was very excited about their tree. I did something great for the environment and saved money, all at the same time.

It was Christmastime, and I was headed back to Chicago after visiting my brother in Iowa. It was snowing as I drove, singing along with the radio. Suddenly, my car started to shut down.

First the radio went, then the heat, and then the car started to slow down no matter how hard I pressed on the accelerator. Luckily, I saw an off-ramp, and my car had just enough juice to get up the hill that led to West Branch, Iowa. My car literally died right in front of a diner.

I found a pay phone and opened my address book to call for help. Sure enough, there was a Ford authorized repair shop right in West Branch—what luck! I called, and the owner said he would send a tow truck in about an hour. He also told me to get some lunch at the diner and to order the Reuben sandwich because it was the best in town.

About an hour later, the tow truck driver came and picked me up. I loved how he did the "country wave" to every car we passed! When I got to the dealership, the repairman told me my car needed a small part, but it would take a couple of hours to fix. His wife was headed to Iowa City to do some last-minute Christmas shopping if I wanted to join her. I didn't hesitate at all! We chatted on the way there and had fun shopping. We got back to the shop, and I paid the $150 repair. They asked me to call when I got home so that they knew I made it safely. When I got home, I opened my wallet to get their business card to call them and found my $150 check back in my wallet with a note that read "Merry Christmas!"

On Christmas morning, a FedEx driver showed up at my door with a package. I opened it up, and there was my address book and a Christmas card that said, "I was cleaning up the diner and found your address book—it looked like it had important papers in it, and I thought you would want it back. Merry Christmas!"

Everyone in West Branch, Iowa, showed me the true meaning of Christmas. I'll never forget their hospitality.

Beth V., Illinois

8

Finding the Bargains

The typical US shopping mall is a wonderful place to enjoy the sights and sounds of the Christmas season. But when it comes to wisely spending your holiday cash according to your holiday spending plan, you'll be surprised how much farther your money will stretch when you stay out of the mall.

Mall Alternatives

Art supply stores. These are great places to find stationery items (mine sells lovely writing paper and matching envelopes by the sheet and also by the ounce or pound), imported art brushes ideal for makeup, fine writing instruments at reasonable prices, photo albums, and all kinds of wonderful portfolios. Chalk, crayons, pads, modeling clay, and packets of construction paper make terrific gifts for kids.

Office supply stores. These stores offer memo books, calendars, pens, and pencils. An appreciated gift for anyone would be a nice box (or other unique container, even a new wastebasket) full of those items you need around the house but can never seem to locate: colored paper clips, staples, tape, labels, Sharpie pens that write on anything, coin wrappers, index cards, Post-it notes, yellow pads or any kind of writing paper, and a personalized rubber stamp. Rubber stamps are fairly cheap and can be specially ordered.

Hardware and home-improvement stores. These are your best bet for all kinds of gadgets and widgets. For the home chef, try an eighteen-inch-long, two-inch wooden dowel for a professional-style rolling pin, a large unglazed terra cotta tile for a pizza/baking stone, or a new paintbrush for a pastry brush. A collection of screws, cup hooks, small tools, etc., can be packed in a small toolbox for a homeowner. Stroll the aisles and you'll get all kinds of great ideas for holiday gifts and supplies, including unusual wrapping materials such as wire and painter's tape. Let your mind wander. Your gift will be quite a hit.

Here are some other alternative shopping locations for your consideration:

- military surplus outlet
- marine supply store
- garden center
- health food store
- damaged freight outlet
- restaurant supply store
- antique store

Online Shopping

As gasoline becomes more expensive and malls become more crowded, the internet is fast becoming the shopping spot of choice. Staying debt-free, however, gets a little tricky as the only wise way to pay for online purchases is with a credit card.

So what makes a retail website really great? First, the site must be user-friendly and easily navigated. To be great it must offer customers good value for the money, excellent customer service, reasonable shipping rates, and a generous return policy.

As convenient as internet shopping can be (no business hours, no parking problems, no cranky salespeople), you have to be aware of the hazards. While some buys may look good, on closer scrutiny they end up not being as great as we first thought. The simplicity of online shopping can blind us to potential pitfalls.

Here are safety tips you should follow to increase the likelihood that your online experience will be satisfying.

Beware of hidden costs. The quoted price may not be the full price. Make sure you read all the fine print, especially regarding shipping and handling charges. Look to see if there are restocking fees on items returned. And who will pay the return shipping costs?

Know the return policy. While many do, merchants are not obligated to accept items for refund, exchange, or credit unless the item is defective.

Exercise discipline. Entering a sixteen-digit credit-card number is so easy that it can pose a serious hazard to your wealth. Keep track of your spending by maintaining a separate list of the gifts you're buying online together with a running balance of your purchases.

Do not use debit cards. Never use a debit card to make an online purchase. It's just too dangerous. Once you input that card's number, two things have happened: (1) You've shouted your number to untold numbers of people in cyberspace, and (2) you've just paid for that purchase. Debit cards do not carry the same consumer protection features required by federal law for credit cards. A thief, using just your debit-card number (no PIN or signature required), could go on an online shopping spree and empty out your checking account and all other accounts attached to it while you sleep. If your bank can prove that you delayed reporting fraud (you didn't check your statements for a few months or watch your account closely online) or were negligent (you wrote your PIN on your card or allowed others to see you input it at an ATM), then you can be left holding the bag.

Use a zero-balance credit card. If you are carrying a balance on a credit-card account, you do not have a grace period. The second you use a credit card that has a revolving balance, you begin to rack up interest charges. If, however, the card you use online has a zero balance at the beginning of the billing cycle, you will have twenty-one days or so (depending on the terms and conditions of your account) to pay before interest charges kick in.

Create your own "debit card." What if I told you there is a way you can have a fully functional debit card without any of the problems and hassles mentioned above? You'd say, "Mary, this is brilliant!" Well, get ready, because that's exactly what I have for you.

Step 1. To do this, you need a credit-card account with a zero balance. This should be a MasterCard or a Visa that has no annual fee.

Step 2. Transfer the money you have set aside for online Christmas shopping into this account. Do this by check or online as you would if you had a balance and sent in the money to pay it off. This will result in your account showing a credit balance. For example, if you send in five hundred dollars, you will see a credit balance of minus five hundred dollars on your next statement or online when you check your account. It's like making a deposit into a bank account, only you are depositing it into your credit-card account.

Step 3. When you shop online, use this "debit card" (which is really a credit card) instead.

Step 4. In two or three days, when you check your account online, you will see the purchase show up on your account as a charge. Your credit balance will be reduced by that amount with no fees or additional charges. If your purchase was for $3.73, your $500 credit balance will be reduced accordingly, to -$496.27.

Step 5. Watch your account as you would any account. If you see a fraudulent charge, you have all of the protection of federal law that regulates credit cards. Call customer service.

Step 6. When your credit balance runs low, deposit additional funds. Just keep in mind that this is not a savings account. A provision in the law states that a creditor must make a good faith effort to refund a credit balance that has remained on an account for more than six months.

Step 7. If you need to get your credit balance refunded, call customer service with your request. By law, they must send it to you in full within seven days of your request.

There you go. And yes, it is brilliant.

Get the best deal. Use a shopping site such as MySimon.com or Froogle.Google.com to comparison shop. Take your time and check thoroughly.

Use online coupons. Before you buy, check sites such as Current Codes.com and RetailMeNot.com for a coupon code for the website you are using. You may find a code for free shipping or an additional discount. Many sites offer a first-time-buyer discount.

Order early. You want to avoid expensive overnight shipping, which can be very steep.

Track your order. Know when the product will ship and how to track your order.

Keep good records. Be sure to print a copy of your order confirmation for your records. Save any email receipts.

General Merchandise

Amazon.com. Amazon began as an online bookstore, but it has expanded tremendously to offer every kind of general merchandise you can imagine through its network of affiliate merchants. Hint: Click on the gold treasure box at the top of the Amazon home page for "Today's Deals." Caution: Like all shopping centers, Amazon is a place you can go broke quickly if you are not extremely disciplined. Keep that spending plan handy at all times.

Overstock.com. Quite possibly this author's favorite place to find high-quality merchandise at rock-bottom prices, Overstock.com hits a home run in most areas of online shopping. Here you will find everything: furniture, bed linens, clothing, jewelry, toys, and household items. Shipping rates are fantastic and change often—even a flat rate for your entire order as low as two dollars every now and then, no matter the size or weight (flat-rate shipping can change from day to day). Customer reviews based on the five-star method offer especially helpful insight.

Shoes

Zappos.com. Imagine a shoe (and clothing) store that carries thousands of name brands and has over ninety thousand styles, six hundred employees, a customer service call center that is staffed 24/7, and two million pairs of shoes in stock and ready for immediate shipment. That is Zappos.com. A unique feature of this shopping site is that customers rate shoes they've purchased and write helpful reviews using the five-star method. Free two-way shipping is standard at Zappos. If you need to return a purchase, simply print a postage-paid label from the Zappos website for a no-questions, postage-paid return on unworn items for up to 365 days. Click "On Sale" for offers on thousands of styles at discounted prices. Beware: Zappos is not a discount site. In exchange for a generous return policy and free two-way shipping, you'll be paying full price.

6pm.com. Part of the Zappos family of companies, 6pm is like a Zappos merchandise outlet. You'll find great deals and excellent customer service. Just know going in that you will pay for shipping both ways and that the return policy is not quite as generous as that of Zappos.com.

Shoebuy.com. This is another shoe site that competes with Zappos and claims to be the world's largest site for shoes, with two billion dollars of inventory. That's a lotta shoes! Shoebuy also offers free two-way shipping and goes the extra mile by including sales tax in the price of shoes. If you find a lower price elsewhere within ten days of purchase, Shoebuy will refund 110 percent of the difference (auction sites don't apply).

DanskoOutlet.com. Dansko offers its factory seconds at bargain prices online. Factory seconds are shoes made in exactly the same way as first-quality merchandise but that have cosmetic flaws. Not every style, size, or color is available. Inventory changes often, so you need to check frequently. Returns and exchanges are allowed, but they must be preapproved.

Books

Half.com. This is a subsidiary of the auction site eBay and a place to buy and sell previously owned books, textbooks, music, movies, and video games. There are no fees to list items for sale. Instead, the company takes a commission of every completed sale.

AbeBooks.com. This is a secure and easy-to-search database for more than 13,500 booksellers. This great selection delivers value for all. Readers find bestsellers, collectors find rare books, students find textbooks, and treasure hunters find books they've been seeking forever. Sales occur seamlessly through checkout with payment made to AbeBooks.com.

BooksPrice.com. No books for sale here. BooksPrice.com is a comparison site for books, DVDs, and CDs. It includes Amazon.com and Half.com. Search results show the price plus cost of shipping, so you know your total before you even proceed to your book site of choice.

Electronics

Woot.com. Wild and just a little wacky, Woot.com is an online store that sells cool stuff cheap—often half the price of the cheapest retail price available online. But rather than a store jammed with all kinds of merchandise, Woot offers only one item. Per day. Woot-life is twenty-four hours. If an item sells out before that time, the site sits idly waiting for the next day.

DeepDiscount.com. This site sells DVDs at discounted prices and ships for free. You may find cheaper prices for isolated titles elsewhere, but overall the prices are great and the selection is extensive.

GotApex.com. This is a portal to the day's hot deals on electronics, computers, and software but also on flowers, jewelry, and housewares from time to time. I don't know how these guys do it, but Apex comes up with deals that are so random and so otherwise unknown that it makes me wonder if they have a sixth sense. The site offers coupon codes and secrets for how to combine discounts, so buyers end up with some pretty amazing deals.

Clothes

SierraTradingPost.com. Just wait until you see all the great bargains on name-brand outerwear, boots, shoes, sandals, sleepwear, and men's and women's clothing for hiking, biking, and camping. Expect to see brands you recognize such as Birkenstock, Earth, Puma, Sebago,

Columbia, and North Face. Discounts of 30 to 70 percent are fairly standard. Need a kayak? They'll send that too, for about one hundred dollars in shipping.

LandsEnd.com. At the home page, click on "Sales" and prepare to be amazed. You'll find serious bargains on women's, men's, and kids' overstocked clothes and merchandise with "itty-bitty flaws" marked down as much as 85 percent. Click on "On the Counter" for low prices—they are posted on Saturday and discounted throughout the week. The company's unconditional guarantee applies even to overstocked and flawed merchandise: "If you're not satisfied with any item, simply return it to us at any time for an exchange or refund of its purchase price."

Bluefly.com. If you're into designer clothing, handbags, and accessories, Bluefly.com is your resource. While the prices aren't cheap by most standards, you will find significant discounts on designer brands such as Prada, Diesel, Gucci, Kate Spade, Coach, and Vera Wang. The selection, variety, and discounts are impressive. Shipping is a flat $7.95 per order.

Specialty

DiscountDance.com. Whether your dancer needs a leotard or tap shoes, here is the online source for discounts. The site carries a wide variety of dancing supplies, including shoes, men's and women's dance clothing, leotards, tights, etc. Beware: Special orders, tights, and sale items cannot be returned. Others may be returned with a receipt within thirty days. For exchanges, expect a $4.95 reshipment charge.

Etsy.com. Think of Etsy as a craft fair where more than ten million talented artisans offer their homemade wares for little more than a song. Finally, the opportunity to own an original piece of art. The site is hip and cool and a great place to find gifts.

Jewelry

SilverJewelryClub.com. This is a site that is almost too crazy to be true. The site features only silver jewelry, offering four pieces of jewelry every ten minutes. If you want an item, you have to quickly fill out your shipping information, and for $6.99 (the cost of shipping and handling), you get a nice piece of silver jewelry worth forty to fifty dollars. That's the pitch. In truth, I have found the jewelry to be of a quality somewhat less than the stated amount but always, in my opinion, more than the cost of shipping. You may have to watch for a long time to come upon something that fits your standards and style, but it's likely to happen.

Crafts

SmileysYarns.com. If you knit or crochet and have all the yarn you need, do not—I repeat, do not—go to this website. With quality name-brand yarn at 50 to 75 percent off retail, the temptation will be too great and you could find yourself committing yarnicide. Prices are cheap on brands you'll recognize such as Bernat, Lion Brand, Cervinia, Rowan, Karabella, and Plymouth (many for just $1.25 per ball), and selections are decent. Beware: Put one skein into your shopping cart and you'll need to add quite a few more to reach the fifty-dollar minimum purchase requirement. Shipping is always a $12.95 flat rate per order, which means you cannot get out of here for less than $62.95. Still, for the serious knitter, this place is like a secret gold mine.

Artbeads.com. Here's an amazing collection of jewelry findings and beads from alphabet to wood, Swarovski to glass, and everything in between, all at wholesale pricing! Order a single bead or dozens. Shipping is always free for orders of ten dollars or more, and there are no minimum purchase requirements. All but clearance items of five dollars or more are refundable for up to sixty days from purchase. Items less than five dollars may be returned for store credit.

Save-on-crafts.com. This is a beautiful website with simple navigation and rich with photographs. You will find deeply discounted craft supplies for scrapbooking, beading, floral design, sewing, quilting, and wedding decorations. Save-on-crafts offers an extensive collection of free projects and inspiration with excellent instructions. Beware: Many items come in multiples of twelve without the option to buy fewer. Watch out or you could end up with a dozen bottles of glue, not the single bottle you intended to buy.

Bargain Finders

MyBargainBuddy.com. This is a helpful site that keeps track of current coupon codes you can use on other sites, features current bargains on the internet, and even sends out an email three times every week to tell you what's new.

Nextag.com. This bargain finder will help you comparison shop for everything from shoes to electronics. It does an excellent job and captures a whole range of prices and sites with customer ratings too. Don't waste your precious time going from site to site. Let this bargain-finding site do that for you.

SundaySaver.com. This site collects the Sunday sales circulars from the newspaper and puts them in one place so you can click through them with your computer mouse. Look up sales by store and by product and run internet product comparisons that pick up the best deals.

NaughtyCodes.com. You will find discount codes here for thousands of online stores. When you click on a store to search codes, the site pulls up the codes and the website for that store.

Miscellaneous

PropertyRoom.com. Started by former police officers, this no-frills site allows you to bid on unclaimed items in the stolen property rooms of police stations.

FatWallet.com. Here's a way you can make some money online. This site will give you a rebate if you go through its portals on your way to shopping at name-brand sites. They get a commission on what you buy and agree to share it with you. FatWallet is more generous than other rebate sites. Check the site for details on how to sign up and which merchants cooperate with them. Another such site is eBates.com.

PlasticJungle.com. Got a gift card you can't use? Trade it for a card you can use or sell it for cash at PlasticJungle.com. You can also buy gift cards at a considerable discount. Make sure you check a card's expiration date and maintenance fees before agreeing to buy it.

An eBay Primer

Think of eBay (ebay.com) as the mother of all garage sales with bargains galore for every purpose imaginable, including Christmas gifts. Millions of transactions occur each day involving individuals, big companies posing as individuals, liquidators posing as home-based businesses, and a few shysters and scam artists thrown into the mix. Want to play? Follow these basics to make sure yours is a pleasant experience.

Do your homework. Learn as much as you can about the item before you bid. Read the description carefully and check measurements. Still have questions? Ask the seller.

Know your prices. Do a quick online search to see if the item or something similar is available new. It's amazing how many people pay more for a used item than a brand-new one at competing retail sites.

Set your boundaries. Based on your research and the condition of the item, determine the most you will pay—the point at which you will stop bidding.

Know your seller. Study the seller's feedback, reports from other buyers who've done business with this seller. Assume you'll be treated the same way.

Know the total cost. Add together your maximum bid, shipping cost, and tax, if any, which will be disclosed up front. This is your full price.

Beware of debt. Like all online payments, you need to handle your eBay transactions with a credit card (not a debit card). And that opens the door to creating new debt. Discipline yourself. The minute you complete that transaction with your credit card, write out a check for the full amount and send it to the credit-card company. Paying the bill will not preclude your ability to dispute the charge should something go awry with your eBay transaction.

Place your bid. Let the competition begin. And good luck!

Outlet Shopping

Remember when "outlet" meant a mostly secret area at the back of a factory, where the manufacturer sold overruns and slightly irregular and discontinued merchandise? Nowadays, "outlet" means a fabulous mall loaded with name-brand stores and promises of bargains galore.

But is it all hype? Do manufacturers really make enough mistakes to fill acres of high-end outlet malls in nearly every area of the country?

Of course, there's plenty of hype, but credible research reveals great bargains on high-quality merchandise plus a remarkably pleasant experience if you know the secrets of how to shop right. Whether you're shopping for yourself or for those on your Christmas list, here are specific guidelines to keep in mind.

Know your outlets. A couple of outlet mall developers maintain detailed and useful websites: PremiumOutlets.com and TangerOutlet .com. For other outlet centers, try doing a web search using your general location—Stockbridge, Massachusetts, for example—plus the word *outlet.* Before you take off on a summer vacation, check these sites for outlet malls that may be on your route.

Wait for the big sales. While outlets regularly shout "Sale!" they follow the same calendar as regular stores. You can count on the best deals around President's Day, Memorial Day, Labor Day, Thanksgiving weekend, and Christmas. January is an especially good time to find bargains at the outlets, as they have to clear space for spring inventory—something that may be of interest if you are really planning ahead on your holiday shopping.

Know your merchandise. The more familiar you are with a manufacturer's merchandise in its regular store, the better you'll be at spotting a true bargain at the outlet. Some goods are manufactured specially for the outlet, and these lines never show up in the regular store. Only a few manufacturers clearly label their outlet lines as such. The Gap, for instance, used to label its outlet line "Gap Factory Store." Now the labels only say "Gap," but you will find three small squares under the logo on the sewn-in label on items that are outlet exclusives.

The only way to know for sure whether you're looking at first-quality, name-brand merchandise or lower-quality goods made specifically for the outlet is to ask. Salesclerks in outlets are usually quite forthcoming and open about their products' origins. As for whether the outlet has the lowest price, that's something you must determine.

One reader wrote that the sweater she bought at the outlet went on sale at the regular store for much less than the outlet price. Due to the outlet store's "all sales final" policy, she was stuck and angry. Buyer beware.

Understand irregulars. If an item is marked "irregular," that means there's a mistake somewhere. It may be quite visible, or it could be difficult to detect. Perhaps that beautiful blazer was cut off-grain. You can't see the flaw, but it will never hang correctly. If you cannot see why an item is marked irregular, ask the clerk. Even then it may be difficult to detect. Proceed with caution.

Use coupons. The major outlet developers (Premium Outlets and Tanger Outlets) have loads of downloadable coupons on their websites for bonus discounts on top of any low prices you will find at the outlet stores. Some offer to send you an email alert for specific sales and offers. You can even sign up to receive discounts on specific name brands. You will need to register at these sites, but the coupons are free.

Join frequent-shopper programs. To get even bigger discounts and saving bonuses, you can join an outlet's frequent-shopper program. Clubs and coupons are typically free, although Tanger charges a one-time ten-dollar membership fee.

Use other discounts. Are you a AAA member? A senior? Many outlets offer discounts for members of various organizations and groups. At Chelsea Premium Outlets, Tuesday is senior discount day.

Inquire about out-of-season merchandise. Want to check out seriously marked-down merchandise? Ask a clerk where they have the out-of-season items. You'll likely be shown to a room in the back of the store where the remains of last season await a willing buyer. Expect to see picked-over goods at rock-bottom prices.

Finally, a word of caution about bargain shopping: The best bargain in the world is way overpriced if you do not need it. Before you make your final decision, step back and make one last assessment. Do you really like the item, or are you justifying the purchase because it's so cheap? Will it be a great gift, or is it more likely to land in your recipient's next garage sale? Be wise, be cautious, and above all pay with cash. That's the way to make outlet shopping work for you.

Gift Cards

Gift cards have taken the US by storm and hang on racks at checkout counters everywhere. These days you can buy gift cards (the modern replacement for the gift certificate) for just about every store imaginable. You can even buy bank gift cards that work in most stores. They are convenient, and for many people, gift cards appear to be the perfect gift solution. They're not. Why? I will tell you.

A gift card is a worthless piece of plastic until purchased and passed through a machine that loads the magnetic strip with the dollar value, the time and date of activation, plus all the details about where the card was purchased and other insider information.

A gift card is not "just like cash." A gift card buys store credit. It is subject to store rules and store policies that vary greatly from one card to another. You cannot exchange it for cash; in fact, you can't even get cash in change if you do not spend it down to the last penny.

Retailers make their own rules. They can impose as many conditions and limitations as their customers will tolerate, provided those conditions are not prohibited by law in the state of issue and are disclosed at the time of purchase. For example, it is unlawful for gift cards issued in California after 1997 to expire (except in some very limited circumstances).

Store gift cards are usually issued fee-free. However, Visa and MasterCard gift cards carry up-front fees of $5.95 or more for the buyer of the card. And if you order by mail? Expect a hefty delivery fee as well.

You may assume that while it is unsafe to send cash through the mail, a gift card is okay to mail. No way! Gift cards are stolen all the time, and unless you have been careful to keep the receipt and the card's identification number, you are out of luck. Even then you or the recipient loses if the thief has spent the balance or the store decides not to honor your documentation. They don't have to.

But here's the most annoying thing: Most gift cards start losing value, some as soon as six months after activation. That can come as a huge shock if you hang on to a gift card. For instance, Visa's Mall of America gift cards purchased before August 22, 2010, came with a plethora of sneaky fees. There's a $2.00 activation fee at the time of purchase. The card magically shrinks by $1.50 per month starting in the thirteenth month after the card's purchase, not when you receive it (this inactivity fee is not applicable to Visa's Mall of America gift cards purchased after August 22, 2010). If you give a gift card you purchased a year ago, it could be worth a lot less than you think. Some cards charge inactivity fees after a period of nonusage has elapsed.

Have you ever wondered what happens to all the money on gift cards that are lost, unused, or just plain forgotten? The research and advisory firm Tower Group predicts that of the $91 billion in gift-card sales in 2010, $2.5 billion (about 3.1 percent) will never be redeemed.[6] Wow! Two and a half billion dollars can't just disappear. So do stores get to keep it? Payments News, an industry watchdog, says that's exactly what happens. After the passage of a sufficient number of years, the retailer can remove the gift-card liability from its books. That means the money is theirs. It is estimated that Walmart could have close to $1 billion of unused gift cards in circulation. Ka-ching! The highest percentage ever recorded for unused gift cards (called "spillage," "spoilage," or "breakage") was 10 percent of all gift cards purchased in 2007.

A gift card is not the same as cash. It's the same as store credit. That's what you are giving as a gift. The store gets to write the rules for how it will handle your recipient and its store credit. And should that store fall into financial trouble, the gift card will become worthless, even if it has no expiration date. Over one hundred million dollars in gift cards was rendered useless or compromised in value in some way in 2008 because of the bankruptcies of Sharper Image, Linens 'n Things, and other failed retailers with outstanding gift cards. Gift-card holders lost another seventy-five million dollars in 2010 due to store and restaurant closings. Did I mention that a gift card is not the same as cash?

Have you ever tried to spend exactly fifty dollars to the penny at any store? It's impossible! Either you have to dig into your pocket to subsidize the cost of your purchase, or you have to leave a few bucks on the card because stores don't give change when you use a gift card.

Another reason to be careful is that gift cards do not command the same respect as real money. They are more easily lost or misplaced than, say, a fifty-dollar bill.

A very useful website, ScripSmart.com, tracks and rates gift-card data from retailers all over the country according to ease of redemption and other criteria. Each gift card is given a numerical rating on a scale of 1 to 100. If you need to know anything about a gift card, this is the place to look. You will also find ratings of each state according to their gift-card laws. You'll be shocked by how many states receive a grade of F.

I have a great idea for a major retailer who's interested in building goodwill among consumers. They should announce that instead of pocketing the windfalls from unused gift cards, they will donate those funds to charity. Now that would get my attention. And you know what? I think I could even warm up to the idea of purchasing gift cards from that merchant. Well, maybe.

Which brings me to this question for all gift-card enthusiasts: What's wrong with a gift of money—beautiful currency? It's always the right color and size, it works absolutely everywhere, and you can be sure your recipient isn't going to accidentally throw it out with all the wrapping paper. Too impersonal, you say? Cold and tacky? I don't think so, but just to be on the safe side, you could always fold those crisp new bills into cute origami shapes to show your recipients just how much you really care.

Google "money origami" to find websites where you can learn quickly how to turn currency into fun gifts that will be far more unique and infinitely more practical than gift cards.

I can hear all of you Starbucks-card lovers screaming in horror. You adore the Starbucks cards (or Target or Bloomies) you get from students, parents, and co-workers. You are a regular customer, you combine your cards, you see them as more precious than cash, and you are more likely to lose your youngest child than your gift cards. Your gift cards give you permission to be frivolous and buy something for yourself you would never buy with cash. Okay, okay. I'm not saying there are no exceptions here.

This is a compromise I can live with: Give a gift card because it is at the top of your recipient's wish list, not because it's an easy default for you.

If you give a gift card:

- check out the conditions before you buy. Avoid cards that charge service fees and do not give back change in cash.
- treat it like cash. If you wouldn't send cash in the mail, don't send a gift card.
- to increase the chances of the gift card actually being used and greatly appreciated, select the store with the recipient's taste and lifestyle in mind, not necessarily yours.
- make sure the recipient is not a child. Cash is better because it's real. The gift-card concept requires abstract thinking.

If you receive a gift card:

- use it right away. Don't save it for later. Sure, it may not have an expiration date, but that store could go out of business before next Tuesday! And the longer you harbor it, the more likely you are to misplace it or simply forget that you have it.
- treat it with respect. Lose it and you're out of luck.

These days as more businesses are filing for bankruptcy, consider this fact: If a company files for a reorganization type of bankruptcy in which it stays in business but under the guidance of the judicial system, which steps in to deal with the company's creditors, it is quite likely that the judge will decree that all outstanding gift cards for that store are null and void. It could happen for the cards you are about to purchase or even for the ones in your wallet, because it's happened many times already. So again, buyers and recipients, beware. Get rid of those cards as quickly as possible because, unfortunately, you need to use them or you might lose them.

If you cannot reasonably use a gift card, trade it, sell it, or give it away. Just don't let it evaporate. Websites such as PlasticJungle.com and Cardpool.com will take it and give you cash back, credit your PayPal account, or give you an Amazon gift card for up to 92 percent of the original gift card's value. Yes, you'll be "losing" money by selling it at a discount. But if you weren't going to use that gift card anyway (or you were going to use it on something you didn't really need), it's probably still a better deal.

Return Policies

Whether you shop in a brick-and-mortar store such as Walmart or Target or an online store such as Amazon or Overstock, the merchant's return policy should be front and center in your mind.

Be forewarned: Returns are not what they used to be. Retailers who collectively lost an estimated $13.95 billion from return fraud[7] have had it up to here with immoral and unethical shoppers who take advantage of return policies. Good, honest consumers like us pay for their crimes in higher prices.

Many big retailers are now depending on software to help them reduce losses that occur when customers abuse store return policies. Companies such as the Retail Equation offer retailers software that allows them to track returns in an effort to reduce fraud. One thing the software looks for is "excessive returns." Of course, we don't know what "excessive" means, as that can vary from one retailer to another, but when that store's threshold is met, the software kicks in and prohibits that customer from making returns until sufficient time has passed. Every time you make a return, the clerk scans your receipt and/or swipes your driver's license. If the company thinks you've been making too many returns, you can be blacklisted without notice. Retailers are able to do all kinds of surveillance because software is cheap and the technology is quite amazing.

I applaud any return policy that says "No way!" to the person who buys a new camcorder on Friday, shoots a wedding on Saturday, and then returns it for a full refund on Monday. I'm happy to support any policy designed to stop the practice of "wardrobing"—buying clothes to be worn to a specific event and then returning them for a full refund the next day.

Sure, tough return policies act to preclude all of us from buying something willy-nilly, assuming that if we change our minds we can just bring it back for a refund whenever we get around to it. And what's wrong with that? Maybe we've become too cavalier when it comes to shopping. Tightening up our selections on the front end is probably a good thing.

I hate to think of all the times I intended to take something back but just didn't get around to it. The unused appliance or clothing item sat in a cupboard or closet through several seasons of procrastination before coming to its final resting place in a yard sale or the Goodwill bag. Perhaps being more keenly aware of a less-than-generous return policy in the beginning would have discouraged me from being so careless with my cash in the first place.

The way I see it, tighter return policies will go a long way to stop immoral shoppers and at the same time make good consumers even better.

Planning to return any holiday gifts? Remember these tips.

Keep your receipts. You need to keep all of your receipts. But you will need more than that. For electronics, make sure the box is sealed—that means not opened, not tested, not used. Clothing? Better have the tags attached and not even a hint that the item has been worn. Many stores now give, in addition to a sales receipt, a gift receipt on request. Always ask for this. Gifts returned with a gift receipt are often treated in a different manner, making the return transaction quite easy.

Watch the calendar. If you miss the window of opportunity to return an item for a refund, you'll be out of luck and reduced to trying to unload the item on eBay. Best Buy has a fourteen-day return period on all things digital. Amazon needs to receive your return within thirty days. Target has a somewhat more generous ninety-day policy for most things but just forty-five days for electronics, DVDs, and so forth, provided they are still sealed in their packaging and you have the receipt. The popular shopping website SmartBargains.com makes no bones about its return policy: "Returns that do not meet our requirements will be sent back to you and no refund will be issued."[8]

Find out about restocking fees. If you've got all your packaging and your dates in order, even then you could be charged a restocking fee (Sears charges 15 percent on a long list of items), ending up with store credit instead of the cash or being tagged a frequent returner. A designation of frequent returner could result in you being banned from returning at certain stores altogether.

Pay with cash whenever possible. Of course, I am referring now to purchases made in walk-in retail stores, not those you make online. Paying with cash is good for your financial future because you can't create debt when you pay with cash. Also, cash sales are not tracked in the store's computer, making it easier for you to make a return for a refund.

Shop thoroughly. The prospect of returns being more carefully scrutinized behooves us to become more careful shoppers. It's easy to get in a rush and skip trying things on in the store, simply taking several colors and sizes on approval, assured that all of it can be returned. Not a good idea. You sure don't want to get stuck with all of those items and be forced to dispose of them at a garage sale for ten cents on the dollar.

Make it your business. Above all, inquire about a store's specific return policies before you make a purchase. If this matter of excessive returns is not addressed in the written policy, ask about it. Inquire how the store determines what is an excessive number of returns.

Several years ago, I started a tradition with my kids that they have outgrown but refuse to let me give up. I purchase twelve pairs of mittens when they go on sale after winter each year, usually at two pair for a dollar. On Thanksgiving weekend, I pin the mittens on a ribbon that I attach to the window in our dining room.

Then I look through the local newspaper and choose free or inexpensive activities in the community that I want to enjoy with my family, such as church Christmas concerts, the community Christmas tree lighting, the hometown Christmas parade, the high school Christmas play, or the community orchestra concert. I write down each person's favorite breakfast food. I choose four activities that serve the needy people in our community, such as serving a meal at a local homeless shelter, taking candy canes to a nursing home, delivering pet food and homemade pet treats to the local animal shelter, or Christmas caroling at the great-grandparents' houses. I also list inexpensive activities we can do at home, such as game and movie nights, story time, homemade pizza making, or cookie baking.

I type each of the twenty-four special moments on individual pages and decorate them. Then I roll them up, tie them with a festive ribbon, and put one in each mitten. Starting on December 1, my kids race to the "Advent mittens" each morning to see what special thing we will be doing that day. After Christmas, we take the mittens to the local homeless shelter.

My children are now both teenagers, but they beg me not to give up the Advent mittens when I suggest they may have outgrown them. Most of the time, they turn down offers from their friends to do things during the holidays, because they don't want to miss a thing. It never ceases to amaze me that knowing you will be having French toast and hot cocoa for supper will keep you excited all day long.

Corena L., Texas

9

Gifts from the Kitchen

It's hard to go wrong giving a delicious, consumable gift. Breads, cakes, cookies, herbed vinegars, flavored mustards, jams, jellies, snacks, candies, chutney, and pickles are just a few of the food items that make highly appreciated gifts.

Hints for Giving Food

A single recipe can be divided into several gifts. Simply arrange pieces of fudge or toffee on a pretty Christmas plate, wrap it in clear cellophane, and top it off with a pretty ribbon or embellishment.

Snack foods can be presented in a small tin or Chinese takeout container. Look for these at any well-stocked craft store. If you don't tell, no one will have to know just how easy and inexpensive these delicious gifts really are.

Write down a favorite family dessert recipe and place it along with all the required ingredients in an appropriate new baking or serving dish. Wrap everything and top it with a big bow.

Present your edibles in special containers: an interesting bottle, a nostalgic candy box, or a pretty jar.

Fill a pretty or comical mug with flavored coffee, tea, or hot chocolate mix. Wrap it along with a holiday-themed, sentimental favorite, or devotional book.

Fill a cookie jar with homemade cookies. Include the recipe.

Wrap up the ingredients and recipe for mulled cider.

Create your own cookie-of-the-month gift (or quarter for the less ambitious among us). Bake one dozen cookies to include in the holiday gift, along with a card announcing that the recipient will receive another dozen each month all year long. This can be one of those gifts that's easy to give but more difficult when it comes to following through, so give cautiously.

Even if you do not cook or bake, you can still give wonderful, inexpensive gifts of food. Buy quantities of nuts, fancy cookies, fresh coffee blends, candies, or dried fruits. Repackage these into small unique containers you've been collecting all year.

A simple cookie cutter in the shape of a star, tree, or gingerbread man can make a great little gift. Lay the cookie cutter in the middle of a piece of clear cellophane. Fill the center of the cookie cutter with tiny candies such as jelly beans. Gather the cellophane and wrap with a bow.

Personalize your food gift with your own label. Millie's Chutney or Minerva's Cookies sound very special.

Attach the recipe to the gift with ribbon, a piece of raffia, or a tasseled cord. Add a spoon or spreader for chutneys or flavored butters.

Here are some of my favorite recipes I've given as gifts over the years.

Cereal Crunch

⅓ cup	white sugar
1¼ teaspoons	cinnamon
¼ cup	butter or margarine
Pinch of salt	
4 cups	Corn Chex, Rice Chex, or Crispix cereal OR 3 cups Bran Chex or Wheat Chex

Mix sugar, cinnamon, and salt and set aside. Melt butter or margarine in large skillet. Add cereal and mix well. Heat over medium heat, stirring until coated (five to six minutes). Sprinkle half of the sugar mixture over the cereal and continue stirring until well coated. Sprinkle with remaining sugar mixture and heat several more minutes. Spread on wax paper or foil to cool. This recipe multiplies well if you have a large skillet.

Yield: 3 to 4 cups.

Santa Claus Cookies

1 package	Nutter Butter (or Vienna Fingers) sandwich cookies
12 ounces	white chocolate wafers or chips*
	Red sprinkles or red-colored sugar
32	vanilla or white chips, not melted
64	semisweet mini chocolate chips
32	red-hot candies

Melt white chocolate. Dip one end of each cookie into melted chocolate. Place on wire racks. For Santa's hat, sprinkle red sugar on top part of chocolate before chocolate hardens. Press one vanilla chip off-center on hat for pom-pom; let stand until set. Dip other end of each cookie into chocolate for Santa's beard, leaving center of cookie uncovered. Place on wire racks. With a dab of melted chocolate, attach semisweet chips for eyes and a red-hot for the nose in the uncovered area. Place on wax paper to set.

Yield: 32 cookies.

---

*Chocolate-melting notes: Melting wafers are chocolate formulated for making candy. They are inexpensive, easy to use, and available at grocery stores, cake and candy supply stores, and craft stores. Chocolate bars and baker's chocolate melt well. Chocolate chips, however, are formulated to resist melting. You can melt them, but it's tricky. Stir in 1 teaspoon vegetable oil for each ounce of chips. Microwave on medium power at thirty-second intervals.

Christmas Crunch

2 cups	white sugar
⅔ cup	light corn syrup
½ cup	water
3 tablespoons	butter
1 teaspoon	vanilla extract
½ teaspoon	baking soda
2 cups	crispy rice cereal
1 cup	cashews

Grease a 10 x 15-inch baking pan. In a large saucepan over medium heat, combine sugar, corn syrup, and water; bring to a boil, stirring constantly until sugar is dissolved. Continue to cook, without stirring, until a candy thermometer reads 300°F. Remove from heat. Stir in butter, vanilla, and baking soda. Add cereal and cashews. Pour into prepared pan and allow to cool. Break into pieces and store in airtight container. Recipe doubles well.

Yield: 3 to 4 cups.

Christmas Walnut Toffee

1 cup	butter
1 cup	white sugar
1 tablespoon	light corn syrup
3 tablespoons	water
1½ cups	chopped walnuts, divided
6 ounces	chocolate chips (your choice)

Grease a 9 x 9-inch baking pan. Melt butter in a large saucepan over medium heat. Add sugar, corn syrup, and water; stir until smooth. Heat to 290°F using a candy thermometer.

When the temperature has been reached, stir in 1 cup walnuts and cook for three more minutes, stirring constantly. Pour into the prepared pan and allow to cool. When the toffee is cool, remove from the pan and place on wax paper. Melt chocolate chips in a metal bowl over a pan of simmering water, or in the microwave, stirring frequently until smooth.

Spread half of the melted chocolate onto one side of the toffee slab and sprinkle with half of the remaining nuts. Allow to cool until set, then repeat on the other side of the toffee. Break into bite-sized pieces when set. Yield: 1 ½ pounds.

Chocolate-Covered Pretzels

Melt your choice of chocolate wafers, bars, or chips. Dip pretzels of any size or shape. Place on wax paper to harden.

SueSue's Chocolate Pecans

1 pound	pecan halves (about 4 cups)
¼ cup	butter
1 teaspoon	salt (or to taste)
12 ounces	chocolate wafers or equivalent

Preheat oven to 350°F. Place butter in a medium bowl. Microwave for thirty seconds on high or until melted. Add pecans and stir until well coated. Spread pecans on a cookie sheet in a single layer and sprinkle generously with salt.

Bake pecans for about ten to twelve minutes or until they just begin to turn a shade darker. Stir several times so they roast evenly. Watch carefully because they can burn very easily.

Meanwhile, in microwave, melt the chocolate in the same bowl you used to melt the butter, following package instructions. Remove pecans from oven and pour into a bowl. Pour chocolate over pecans and stir to coat thoroughly. Drop by spoonfuls onto wax paper. If you want, you can break up some of the pecans to make smaller portions.

Once completely cooled, place in airtight containers or zip-type bags. Variations: You can make this with white chocolate or almond bark too. Yield: a lot—and they're fabulous!

Almond Crunch

1 cup	butter (no substitutes)
1¼ cups	sugar
2 tablespoons	light corn syrup
2 tablespoons	water
1 cup	chopped or slivered almonds
12 ounces	milk chocolate chips

Preheat oven to 375°F. Arrange almonds in a single layer on a baking sheet. Toast until lightly browned, approximately five minutes.

Line a jelly roll pan with foil. In a heavy saucepan, combine butter, sugar, corn syrup, and water. Cook over medium heat, stirring constantly, until mixture boils. Boil, without stirring, to hard crack stage, 300°F. Remove from heat.

Working quickly, stir in almonds and pour mixture into foil-lined jelly roll pan; tip pan from side to side to spread candy evenly in pan. Sprinkle chocolate chips over candy brittle. Let stand about five minutes or until shiny and soft. Spread chocolate evenly over candy. Cool to room temperature, then refrigerate for one hour. Break into bite-sized pieces.

Note: Best when made on a dry day. If it's raining, this will not get as brittle as it should.

Easy Candy Cane Fudge

20 ounces	white chocolate chunk-sized chips (12-ounce packages of small white chocolate chips may be substituted)
1 14-ounce can	sweetened condensed milk
½ teaspoon	peppermint extract
1½ cups	crushed candy canes
1 dash	red or green food coloring

Line an 8 x 8-inch baking pan with aluminum foil; grease the foil. Combine chocolate and sweetened condensed milk in a saucepan over medium heat.

Stir frequently until almost melted. Remove from heat and continue to stir until smooth. When chips are completely melted, stir in peppermint extract, food coloring, and crushed candy canes. Spread mixture evenly in prepared pan. Chill for two hours, then cut into squares.

Yield: 40 to 45 pieces.

Holiday Fudge

12 large	marshmallows
2 cups	white sugar
1 6-ounce can	evaporated milk
6 ounces	semisweet chocolate chips
½ cup	butter
1 teaspoon	vanilla
1 cup	chopped walnuts (optional)

Lightly butter an 8 x 8-inch glass pan. Combine chocolate chips, walnuts, and butter in a mixing bowl and set aside. In a large saucepan, combine marshmallows, sugar, and evaporated milk over medium heat and stir constantly until mixture comes to a boil. Boil exactly six minutes (time this carefully) and remove from stove. Pour this hot mixture over ingredients in the bowl. Stir to combine and then beat by hand or on low speed with an electric mixer for exactly twenty minutes. Stir in vanilla. Pour into the glass pan. Allow to cool and set. Cut into squares.

Yield: 40 to 45 pieces.

Note: If this does not turn out perfectly, you likely did not believe me about exact timing. Try again. It's that good and not that expensive to make.

Holiday Spiced Nuts

2 cups	walnut halves
1 cup	hazelnuts
1 cup	whole unsalted cashews
1 cup	pecan halves
3 tablespoons	butter
1 teaspoon	ground anise
1 teaspoon	ground cinnamon
1 teaspoon	coarse black pepper
½ teaspoon	freshly grated nutmeg
1 cup	smoked almonds

Heat a large skillet and cook walnuts, hazelnuts, cashews, and pecans over moderate heat for seven to eight minutes, stirring constantly until golden and well toasted. Do not leave unattended as nuts can burn quickly. Transfer nuts to a plate and return pan to stove. Add butter to the pan in small pieces. Add anise, cinnamon, pepper, and nutmeg and stir for one minute to allow butter to become infused. Turn off heat. Add toasted nuts and smoked almonds to the skillet. Gently stir until all ingredients are incorporated. Allow to cool.

Yield: 6 cups.

Slow Cooker Sugared Nuts

The unusual steps in this recipe ensure that the nuts are crisp and perfectly glazed, so follow these instructions carefully.

½ pound	pecan halves
½ pound	shelled walnuts
½ cup	butter, melted
½ cup	powdered sugar
¼ teaspoon	ground allspice
⅛ teaspoon	ground cloves
1½ teaspoons	ground cinnamon
¼ teaspoon	ground ginger

Preheat a 3½- to 4-quart slow cooker, uncovered, on high for fifteen minutes. In warmed slow cooker, combine nuts and butter and stir well. Add powdered sugar, stirring to coat evenly. Cover slow cooker and cook on high for fifteen minutes. Reduce heat to low and cook uncovered, stirring occasionally, until nuts are coated with a crisp glaze, about two hours. Transfer nuts to a large bowl. In a small bowl, combine spices. Sift them over the nuts, stirring to coat evenly. Let cool and store in an airtight container.

Yield: 6 cups.

Slow Cooker Chex Mix

This classic combination of cereal, nuts, butter, and seasonings cooks in your slow cooker so you don't have to watch it or stir it while it's baking.

3 cups	thin pretzel sticks
4 cups	Wheat Chex cereal
4 cups	Cheerios cereal
12 ounces	salted peanuts
½ teaspoon	garlic salt
½ teaspoon	celery salt
½ teaspoon	seasoned salt
¼ cup	butter, melted
⅓ cup	grated Parmesan cheese

Combine all ingredients in a 4- or 5-quart slow cooker and stir gently until well mixed and cereal, pretzels, and peanuts are coated with butter, cheese, and spices. Cover and cook on low for three to four hours, stirring twice during cooking. Remove lid during last half hour of cooking to let the mix dry.

Yield: 12 cups.

Peppermint Bark

8 ounces	white chocolate, chopped
4	red-and-white peppermint sticks OR 6-inch candy canes, crushed
2 drops	peppermint oil or extract

Line a 13 x 17-inch cookie sheet with sides with parchment paper or a nonstick baking mat. Melt white chocolate in a double boiler or microwave. When chocolate is melted, stir in peppermint oil. Stir in all but 2 tablespoons of the crushed peppermint pieces and spread the mixture on the cookie sheet, about ¼-inch thick. It will not fill the pan completely. Sprinkle the reserved peppermint pieces over the top. Let set at room temperature until hardened, about two hours (or refrigerate for thirty minutes to harden more quickly). Use your hands to break into pieces. ' Store in an airtight container for up to two weeks.

Yield: 3 to 4 cups.

Lemon Sugar

3	lemons
2 cups	white sugar

Using a zester or fine grater, remove only the zest from all three lemons (no white pith). Stir zest with sugar in a mixing bowl; then spread mixture out on a cookie sheet and let dry for about one hour. Place in an airtight container. Add this tag: "Lemon sugar gives a cup of tea that perfect zing!"

Yield: 2 cups.

Vanilla Sugar

1	vanilla bean, split in half lengthwise and crosswise
4 cups	white sugar

In a large container with an airtight closure, place 2 cups of sugar. Add the bean quarters and cover with the remaining 2 cups of sugar. Close tightly. Place in a cool, dark place. Twice a day shake the container to distribute the vanilla essence. Continue the process for at least one week and up to three weeks. Place in an airtight container. Add this tag: "Vanilla sugar: Use as regular, granulated sugar (for instance, in coffee or cereal)."

Yield: 4 cups.

Almond Coffee Creamer

¾ cup	powdered sugar
¾ cup	powdered non-dairy creamer
1 teaspoon	ground cinnamon
1 teaspoon	almond extract

Mix all ingredients in a bowl. Place in an airtight container. Add this tag: "Almond coffee creamer: Add to coffee in place of non-dairy creamer and sugar."

Yield: 1½ cups.

Chai Tea Mix

1½ cups	instant tea powder
2 cups	powdered non-dairy creamer
½ cup	dry milk powder
1 cup	powdered sugar
¼ cup	brown sugar
1 teaspoon	ground ginger
1 teaspoon	ground cinnamon
1 teaspoon	ground cloves
1 teaspoon	ground cardamom
1 teaspoon	ground allspice
1 teaspoon	vanilla powder

In a food processor, combine instant tea, powdered creamer, dry milk powder, powdered sugar, and brown sugar. Add ginger, cinnamon, cloves, cardamom, allspice, and vanilla powder. Process for two minutes. Place in an airtight container. Add this tag: "Chai tea mix: To serve, place 4 teaspoons in a cup and fill with hot water. Stir and enjoy!"

Yield: 3½ cups.

Bavarian Mint Coffee Mix

¼ cup	instant nonfat powdered dry milk
⅓ cup	white sugar
¼ cup	instant coffee
2 tablespoons	unsweetened cocoa powder
2	hard peppermint candies, crushed

Combine all ingredients in a food processor or blender. Process until mixed. Place in an airtight container. Add this tag: "Bavarian mint coffee mix: To serve, combine 3 tablespoons with 1 cup boiling water. Stir to blend. Ahhh!"

Yield: 1 cup.

Friendship Tea

1 cup	powdered Tang
½ cup	instant lemonade drink mix
1½ cups	white sugar
1 cup	instant tea (unsweetened)
2 teaspoons	ground cinnamon
1 teaspoon	ground cloves

Pour all ingredients into a large bowl and mix well. Place in an airtight container. Add this tag: "Friendship tea: To serve, combine 3 teaspoons with 1 cup boiling water. Stir and enjoy!"

Yield: 4 cups.

Cappuccino Mix

1 cup	powdered instant creamer
1 cup	cocoa
⅔ cup	instant coffee granules
½ cup	white sugar
½ teaspoon	cinnamon
¼ teaspoon	nutmeg

Combine all ingredients. Place in an airtight container. Add this tag: "Cappuccino mix: To serve, place 4 teaspoons in a cup and add boiling water. Stir well. Enjoy!"

· Yield: 3 ½ cups.

Mocha Mix

1½ cups	white sugar
1 cup	instant coffee granules
1 cup	powdered non-dairy creamer
¼ cup	cocoa
½ teaspoon	salt
½ teaspoon	cinnamon (optional)

Mix ingredients thoroughly. Place in an airtight container. Add this tag: "Mocha mix: To serve, combine 2 tablespoons with 1 cup boiling water. Stir and enjoy!"

Yield: 3 to 4 cups.

When I was a little girl growing up in Kansas in the late seventies, I had a brother named Bob who was twelve years older than me. I rarely saw him due to our age difference. He was very sick his whole life, suffering from diabetes. At the time, he was working with a cleaning crew at the bank where my dad worked. Even at seven years old, I knew he had very little money. For Christmas, he gave me a giant roll of paper that he was allowed to take from the bank and a box of sixty-four crayons. I loved that gift. I could roll the paper out to twenty feet and draw giant pictures.

Gifts in our house were elaborate and went on forever, and I remember few of them. But I will never forget the paper and the crayons from my brother Bob. Contact between us as adults was rare, and he passed away in 1996. I will never forget how hard he must have tried to think of a gift for his baby sister.

℞ Kelly B., Georgia

In August, my daughter and I make out our Christmas lists. These are not for things we want but rather the people we want to bless from our kitchen. We plan the different treats for simplicity and figure out what ingredients and quantities we will need. Each week we buy a few things for the "holiday shelf" when we do our food shopping, and by the week after Thanksgiving we have all that we need.

We start on Black Friday (for us, a go-nowhere, spend-nothing day). We bake, cook, jar, tray, and package all of our treats using containers purchased at after-Christmas sales from the previous year. By the end of the week we are done and all the mailed gifts are sent. Over the next weeks before Christmas, we deliver the local gifts and enjoy a stress-free, no-malls, no-crowds Christmas.

℞ Michele B., email

"Yep, worldwide virtual Christmas via high-speed broadband. Sorry, boys, I won't be needing your service anymore. I'm gonna miss ya!"

10

Gifts in a Jar

Strictly speaking, you can make a gift from anything you can stuff into a glass canning jar. Embellish it with fabric, ribbon, or raffia; add a tag that gives the recipient specific instructions on what to do with the contents; and you've just made a jar gift. Some jar gifts contain ingredients with instructions for the recipient to finish the product; others are finished and ready to go.

The great thing about jar gifts, especially when the contents are edible, is that they become perfect repeat performers. People of all ages love these gifts, so you can give them year after year with confidence they will be received with rave reviews. You can buy new canning jars for about twelve dollars a dozen at grocery stores, department stores such as Walmart, and craft stores. Regardless of the jar size (this will vary from one recipe to another, although the recipes in this book use the quart size unless otherwise specified), always use widemouthed canning jars. You can also purchase replacement rings and lids for old jars. Always use new lids.

Jars also come in smaller sizes that are perfect for spice blends, herbed mixes, potpourri, and bath salts. Always prepare a tag for the jar gift that explains what it is and how to use it.

You can make jar gifts one at a time or take care of your entire gift list in one marathon-like event using the assembly line method. I've lined up as many as two dozen jars at a time and found that the assembly goes quickly and efficiently. Just make sure that you measure carefully and, in the case of layered jars, pack the contents tightly so there's no room for shifting.

Jars containing the dry ingredients for cookies or other sweets can be stored in a cool, dark place for up to six months. To keep longer, store in the refrigerator or freezer.

You will help your recipients when you add a "best if used by" date. Of course, this will be determined by how long you have stored the finished product prior to presentation. It is best to err on the side of caution, suggesting the item be used within three months.

Any item given in a jar can be dressed up and personalized. Cut a six-inch square of fabric with pinking shears. Center the fabric over the lid. Using a hot glue gun, attach the fabric to the lid. Tie a ribbon around the rim and finish with a bow. Cut a circle of paper to fit the jar lid, use gold rope or string, and a wax seal with an impression of your initial. The gift tag can describe the contents with suggested uses and include the recipe.

Jar gifts are perfect for singles, kids (even young children can follow the directions and make cookies with some adult supervision), seniors, teachers, co-workers—everyone on your list. The only problem you may encounter is a recipient who simply cannot bear to use the jar gift because it is so beautiful. In that case, I suggest you give another on the next appropriate occasion. And you know what that means? You've started a tradition!

Cookies, Brownies, and Sweet Treats

Layered to look like sand art, these fabulous mixes make the perfect gift for anyone on your list.

Chocolate Chip Cookies

½ cup	white sugar
½ cup	chopped pecans
1 cup	chocolate chips
1 cup	firmly packed brown sugar .
2 ½ cups	all-purpose flour mixed with 1 teaspoon baking soda and ¼ teaspoon salt

Layer ingredients in the order given, pressing each layer firmly in place before adding the next ingredient. Everything will fit if you are diligent to pack each layer tightly, particularly the brown sugar and flour.

Attach this message to the jar:

—— Chocolate Chip Cookies ——

Empty contents of jar into large mixing bowl and thoroughly blend. Add ¾ cup softened butter or margarine (not diet or tub variety), 1 egg, and 1 teaspoon vanilla. Mix well. Shape into walnut-sized balls and place two inches apart on a greased cookie sheet. Bake at 350°F for seven to ten minutes or until just slightly golden. Do not overbake. Cool ten minutes on baking sheet. Remove to racks to finish cooling. These cookies will not firm up until completely cooled. Yield: 2½ dozen.

Trail Mix Cookies

½ cup	packed brown sugar
½ cup	white sugar
¾ cup	wheat germ
⅓ cup	quick-cooking oats
1 cup	raisins
⅓ cup	packed flaked coconut
½ cup	all-purpose flour mixed with 1 teaspoon baking powder

Layer ingredients in the order given, pressing each layer firmly in place before adding the next ingredient. It will be a very tight fit. Keep gift refrigerated.

Attach this message to the jar:

——— Trail Mix Cookies ———

Keep jar refrigerated until ready to bake. Empty contents of jar into large mixing bowl and thoroughly blend. Add ½ cup soft butter; 1 egg, slightly beaten; and 1 teaspoon vanilla. Mix until completely blended. Shape into walnut-sized balls and place two inches apart on a greased cookie sheet. Bake at 350°F for twelve to fourteen minutes or until edges are lightly browned. Cool five minutes on baking sheet. Remove cookies to racks to finish cooling. Yield: 2½ dozen.

Easiest Ever Chocolate Chip Cookies

1⅔ cups	all-purpose flour
¾ teaspoon	baking soda
½ cup	white sugar
2 cups	semisweet chocolate chips
½ cup	packed brown sugar

Combine the flour, baking soda, white sugar, and chocolate chips. Place one half of the mixture in a jar and pack firmly. Place the brown sugar on top, again packing firmly. Finish with the remaining flour mixture on top.

Attach this message to the jar:

——— Easiest Ever Chocolate Chip Cookies ———

Empty contents of jar into large bowl. In separate bowl, combine ¾ cup of softened butter, 2 eggs, and 1 teaspoon vanilla. Beat until creamy. Add to dry mixture. Drop by spoonfuls onto an ungreased cookie sheet and bake at 375°F for eight to ten minutes. Yield: 2 dozen.

Reese's Peanut Butter Cup Cookies

¾ cup white sugar

¼ cup packed brown sugar

1¾ cups all-purpose flour mixed with 1 teaspoon baking powder and ½ teaspoon baking soda

8 large Reese's Peanut Butter Cups cut into ½-inch pieces (wrap in plastic wrap)

Layer ingredients in order given, pressing each layer firmly in place before adding the next ingredient. The cut candy pieces should be wrapped in plastic wrap and then added as the final layer. This will keep them fresh and the other ingredients dry until use.

Attach this message to the jar:

———— Reese's Peanut Butter Cup Cookies ————

Remove candies from jar, discard plastic wrap, and set aside. Empty contents of jar into large mixing bowl; stir to combine. Add ½ cup softened butter; 1 egg, slightly beaten; and 1 teaspoon vanilla. Mix until completely blended. Stir in candies. Roll dough into walnut-sized balls and place two inches apart on a lightly greased cookie sheet. Bake at 375°F for twelve to fourteen minutes or until edges are lightly browned. Cool five minutes on baking sheet. Remove to wire racks to cool completely. Yield: 2½ dozen.

Oatmeal Raisin Spice Cookies

¾ cup packed brown sugar

½ cup white sugar

¾ cup raisins

2 cups quick-cooking oats

1 cup all-purpose flour mixed with 1 teaspoon cinnamon, ½ teaspoon nutmeg, 1 teaspoon baking soda, and ½ teaspoon salt

Layer ingredients in order given, pressing each layer firmly in place before adding the next ingredient.

Attach this message to the jar:

———— Oatmeal Raisin Spice Cookies ————
Empty contents of jar into large mixing bowl; stir to combine. Add ¾ cup softened butter (not diet margarine); 1 egg, slightly beaten; and 1 teaspoon vanilla. Mix until completely blended. Roll heaping spoonfuls into balls and place two inches apart on a lightly greased cookie sheet. Bake at 350°F for eleven to thirteen minutes or until edges are lightly browned. Cool five minutes on baking sheet. Remove to wire racks to cool completely. Yield: 3 dozen.

Orange Slice Cookies

¾ cup	white sugar
½ cup	packed brown sugar
1¾ cups	all-purpose flour mixed with 1 teaspoon baking powder and ½ teaspoon baking soda
1½ cups	orange slice candies, quartered (wrap in plastic wrap)

Layer ingredients in order given, pressing each layer firmly in place before adding the next ingredient.

Attach this message to the jar:

———— Orange Slice Cookies ————
Remove candies from jar, discard plastic wrap, and set aside. Empty contents of jar into large mixing bowl; stir to combine. Add ½ cup softened butter; 1 egg, slightly beaten; and 1 teaspoon vanilla. Mix until completely blended. Stir in orange candies. Roll dough into walnut-sized balls and place two inches apart on a lightly greased cookie sheet. Bake at 375°F for twelve to fourteen minutes or until edges are lightly browned. Cool five minutes on baking sheet. Remove to wire racks to cool completely. Yield: 2½ dozen.

Chocolate-Covered Raisin Cookies

¾ cup   white sugar

½ cup   packed brown sugar

1 cup   chocolate-covered raisins

½ cup   milk chocolate chips

1¾ cups   all-purpose flour mixed with 1 teaspoon baking powder and 1 teaspoon salt

Layer ingredients in order given, pressing each layer firmly in place before adding the next ingredient.

Attach this message to the jar:

—— Chocolate-Covered Raisin Cookies ——

Empty contents of jar into large mixing bowl; stir to combine. Add ½ cup softened butter; 1 egg, slightly beaten; and 1 teaspoon vanilla. Mix until completely blended. Roll heaping spoonfuls into balls and place two inches apart on a lightly greased cookie sheet. Bake at 375°F for thirteen to fifteen minutes or until tops are very lightly browned. Cool five minutes on baking sheet. Remove to wire racks to cool completely. Yield: 2½ dozen.

Hawaiian Cookies

⅓ cup   white sugar

½ cup   packed brown sugar

⅓ cup   packed flaked coconut

⅔ cup   chopped macadamia nuts

⅔ cup   chopped dates

2 cups   all-purpose flour mixed with 1 teaspoon baking soda and 1 teaspoon baking powder

Layer ingredients in order given, pressing each layer firmly in place before adding the next ingredient.

Attach this message to the jar:

——— Hawaiian Cookies ———

Empty contents of jar into large mixing bowl; stir to combine. Add ½ cup softened butter; 1 egg, slightly beaten; and 1 teaspoon vanilla. Mix until completely blended. Roll dough into walnut-sized balls and place two inches apart on a lightly greased cookie sheet. Press cookie down slightly with the heel of your hand. Bake at 350°F for eleven to thirteen minutes or until edges are lightly browned. Cool five minutes on baking sheet. Remove to wire racks to cool completely. Yield: 2½ dozen.

Raisin Crunch Cookies

½ cup	white sugar
½ cup	raisins
1¼ cups	packed flaked coconut
1 cup	crushed cornflakes
¾ cup	packed brown sugar
½ cup	quick-cooking oats
1¼ cups	all-purpose flour mixed with 1 teaspoon baking soda and 1 teaspoon baking powder

Layer ingredients in order given, pressing each layer firmly in place before adding the next ingredient.

Attach this message to the jar:

——— Raisin Crunch Cookies ———

Empty contents of jar into large mixing bowl; stir to combine. Add 1 cup softened butter; 1 egg, slightly beaten; and 1 teaspoon vanilla. Mix until completely blended. Roll dough into walnut-sized balls and place two inches apart on a lightly greased cookie sheet. Bake at 350°F for ten to twelve minutes or until edges are lightly browned. Cool five minutes on baking sheet. Remove to wire racks to cool completely. Yield: 3 to 4 dozen.

Dreamsicle Cookies

½ cup	Tang drink powder
¾ cup	white sugar
1½ cups	white chocolate chips
1¾ cups	all-purpose flour mixed with ½ teaspoon baking soda and ½ teaspoon baking powder

Layer ingredients in order given, pressing each layer firmly in place before adding the next ingredient.

Attach this message to the jar:

—— Dreamsicle Cookies ——

Empty contents of jar into large mixing bowl; stir to combine. Add ½ cup softened butter; 1 egg, slightly beaten; and 1 teaspoon vanilla. Mix until completely blended. Roll heaping spoonfuls into balls and place two inches apart on a lightly greased cookie sheet. Bake at 375°F for twelve to fourteen minutes or until tops are very lightly browned. Cool five minutes on baking sheet. Remove to wire racks to cool completely. Yield: 2½ dozen.

M&M Cookies

1¼ cups	white sugar
1¼ cups	M&M's
2 cups	all-purpose flour mixed with ½ teaspoon baking soda and ½ teaspoon baking powder

Layer ingredients in order given, pressing each layer firmly in place before adding the next ingredient.

Attach this message to the jar:

—— M&M Cookies ——

Empty contents of jar into large mixing bowl; stir to combine. Add ½ cup softened butter; 1 egg, slightly beaten; and 1 teaspoon vanilla. Mix until completely blended. Roll dough into walnut-sized balls and place two inches apart on a lightly greased cookie sheet. Bake at 375°F for twelve to fourteen minutes or until edges are lightly browned. Cool five minutes on baking sheet. Remove to wire racks to cool completely. Yield: 2½ dozen.

Cranberry Pistachio Biscotti

¾ cup dried cranberries or cherries

¾ cup shelled green pistachios

2 cups all-purpose unbleached flour mixed with ½ teaspoon cinnamon and 2 teaspoons baking powder

⅔ cup white sugar

Layer ingredients in jar in order given. Tap the jar gently on the countertop to settle each layer before adding the next, adding dried fruits or pistachios to fill any gaps. Make sure you compress the flour well using your fingers or the end of a wooden spoon.

Attach this message to the jar:

—— Cranberry Pistachio Biscotti ——

Beat ⅓ cup butter on medium speed for thirty seconds. Add 2 eggs and beat on medium until well combined. Using a wooden spoon, stir in contents of jar until just combined. Divide into two loaves on a cookie sheet. Chill dough if necessary to make it easier to handle. Each loaf should be about nine inches long and two inches wide. Bake at 375°F for twenty-five to thirty minutes or until a toothpick inserted in the center comes out clean. Cool on baking sheet for one hour. Cut each loaf diagonally into ½-inch thick slices using a serrated bread knife. Place slices on an ungreased cookie sheet. Bake at 325°F for eight minutes, then turn over and bake for an additional eight to ten minutes more or until dry and crisp. Transfer to wire rack to cool. Yield: 32 cookies.

Sand Art Brownies

¾ teaspoon	salt
1⅛ cups	flour, divided
⅓ cup	cocoa powder
⅔ cup	packed brown sugar
⅔ cup	white sugar
½ cup	chocolate chips
½ cup	white chocolate chips
½ cup	walnuts or pecans

Divide the flour and layer ingredients in the order given (and put second half of flour between the cocoa and brown sugar), pressing each layer firmly in place before adding the next ingredient.

Attach this message to the jar:

———— Sand Art Brownies ————

Empty contents of jar into large bowl and mix well. Add 1 teaspoon vanilla, ⅔ cup vegetable oil, and 3 eggs. Beat until just combined. Pour batter into a greased 9 x 9-inch baking pan. Bake at 350°F for twenty to twenty-five minutes. Yield: 2½ dozen brownies.

Butterscotch Brownies

½ cup	flaked coconut
½ cup	granulated sugar
2 cups	packed brown sugar
2 cups	all-purpose flour mixed with 1½ teaspoons baking powder and ¼ teaspoon salt

Layer ingredients in the order given, pressing each layer firmly in place before adding the next ingredient.

Attach this message to the jar:

———— Butterscotch Brownies ————

Empty contents of jar into large mixing bowl and thoroughly blend. Add ¾ cup butter or margarine softened at room temperature (do not use diet margarine). Mix in 2 eggs, slightly beaten, and 2 teaspoons vanilla. Mix until completely blended. Spread batter into a greased 9 x 13-inch metal pan. Bake at 375°F for twenty-five minutes. Cool fifteen minutes in baking pan. Cut brownies into 1½-inch squares. Cool completely in pan. Yield: 2 dozen.

Cinnamon Pancakes

3 cups	all-purpose flour
4 teaspoons	ground cinnamon
2¼ tablespoons	granulated sugar
2 tablespoons	baking powder
1¼ teaspoons	salt

Layer ingredients in the order given, pressing each layer firmly in place before adding the next ingredient.

Attach this message to the jar:

—— Cinnamon Pancakes ——

Empty contents of jar into large bowl. Mix thoroughly. Measure out 1⅓ cups of the mix and set aside. Return the balance of the mix to the jar for future use. In a medium bowl, combine ¾ cup milk, 1 egg, and 2 tablespoons vegetable oil. Add mix. Whisk until moistened but still lumpy. Prepare pancakes as usual. Yield: 5 to 6 small pancakes.

119

Savory Treats

Grilling Spices

3 tablespoons	whole coriander seeds
3 tablespoons	cumin seeds
3 tablespoons	dill seeds
3 tablespoons	yellow mustard seeds
6 tablespoons	whole fennel seeds
6 tablespoons	sugar
3 tablespoons	salt
1½ teaspoons	fresh ground pepper

Combine all seeds in a skillet over medium heat. Toast, shaking pan, about four minutes. Using a spice grinder or food processor, coarsely grind seeds. Transfer to a small bowl. Add sugar, salt, and pepper. Stir well to combine. Makes about 1½ cups.

Attach this message to the jar:

—— Grilling Spices ——

These grilling spices give meat, fish, or poultry an intensely flavorful, slightly crunchy outer layer while sealing in the meat's juices. Simply rub in the spices and cook—no waiting time is required. Keep jar tightly closed and store at room temperature for up to six months.

Cajun Spices

¾ cup	salt
¼ cup	ground cayenne pepper
2 tablespoons	ground white pepper
2 tablespoons	ground black pepper
2 tablespoons	paprika
2 tablespoons	onion powder
2 tablespoons	garlic powder

Put each ingredient into a separate cup or small bowl. While holding a pint canning jar at an angle, add ingredients to create a sand art look. The salt and cayenne may be divided into smaller portions and used to separate other spices, creating more stripes.

Attach this message to the jar:

——— Cajun Spices ———
Can be used on potatoes, eggs, and meat. Enjoy!

Corn Bread

1 cup	yellow cornmeal
1 cup	flour
¼ cup	white sugar (optional)
4 teaspoons	baking powder
½ teaspoon	salt

Sift together all ingredients and place in jar.

Attach this message to the jar:

——— Corn Bread ———
Empty contents of jar into bowl. Add 1 egg, 1 cup milk, and 4 tablespoons shortening. Beat until smooth (about one minute with whisk). Pour batter into a greased 8 x 8-inch baking pan. Bake at 425°F for twenty minutes or until a knife inserted at the center comes out clean. Yield: 9 to 12 pieces.

Southwestern Fiesta Dip Mix

½ cup	dried parsley
⅓ cup	onion flakes
¼ cup	dried chives
⅓ cup	chili powder
¼ cup	ground cumin
¼ cup	salt

In a large bowl, combine the spices and fill small jars.

Attach this message to the jars:

—— Southwestern Fiesta Dip Mix ——

Combine 3 tablespoons of the dip mix with 1 cup mayonnaise (regular or low-fat) and 1 cup sour cream (or yogurt). Whisk until smooth. Refrigerate for two to four hours. Serve with tortilla chips or fresh vegetables. Yield: 2 cups.

Hearty Friendship Soup

⅓ cup	beef or chicken bouillon granules
¼ cup	onion flakes
½ cup	split peas
½ cup	alphabet pasta (any small pasta is fine)
¼ cup	barley
½ cup	lentils
⅓ cup	non-instant white rice
	Tricolor spiral pasta

Layer ingredients in the order given. A funnel makes the job easier. Add enough tricolor spiral pasta to fill the jar.

Attach this message to the jar:

—— Hearty Friendship Soup ——

In large kettle, brown 1 pound ground beef (or stew beef or chicken that has been cut into bite-sized pieces in a little olive or vegetable oil). Remove the tricolor pasta from the jar and set aside. Add contents of jar to a pot containing 12 cups water. Bring the soup to a boil and simmer forty-five minutes. Add the tricolor pasta and simmer fifteen minutes longer. Serve with your favorite bread or rolls and a tossed salad. Yield: 8 servings.

Nonedible Gifts

Spring in a Jar

There's nothing quite like crocuses or hyacinths opening on the breakfast table to cheer up a late January morning. In this jar gift, you provide everything necessary for your recipient to water-force beautiful flowers that will bloom indoors—in the dead of winter.

Bulbs that are easily water-forced—hyacinths, crocuses, paperwhites, narcissus, and tulips—are generally available summer through Labor Day. If you wait until December to get your supplies, you will be out of luck.

Store bulbs in paper bags in a cold (around 45°F), dark place until you are ready to make your jar gift. Note: The refrigerator is perfect, provided bulbs are not sharing space with fruit. Fruits emit a gas that is harmful to the bulbs.

These are the items you will need for the jar gift:

> 1-quart widemouthed canning jar with lid
> Charcoal, gravel-sized (available in the garden department)
> Small pebbles or gravel
> Bulb(s) of choice
> Small brown paper bag
> Twine or ribbon
> Other garden items (optional)

Place 1 to 2 inches of charcoal in the bottom of the jar. Follow with a layer of gravel or pebbles that are bone dry. The jar should be about half full. Wrap the bulb in a small brown paper bag, tie loosely with twine or ribbon, and set on top of gravel. Add other garden-theme items such as gloves or a packet of seeds for visual effect. These items are not part of the forcing process, and you should include a note to remove these items upon opening the gift.

Store uncovered in a cold, dark place until presentation.

Attach this message to the jar:

Remove everything from the jar except the pebbles and charcoal. Remove the bulb from the bag and push it root side down into the pebbles just a little bit so it sits securely.

Fill the jar with water until the water almost touches the bottom of the bulb. Place the uncovered jar inside a brown paper grocery bag and keep it in a cool (50°F to 55°F) place.

Check often to make sure the water level remains steady. If no roots appear, add a little more water; if mold appears, keep the water level a bit lower. Roots should sprout in about two weeks, and top shoots will appear shortly thereafter.

When crocus shoots reach one inch (two inches in the case of hyacinths, narcissus, paperwhites, or tulips), take the jar from the grocery bag and place it in a cool, lighted place where you can admire its emerging beauty.

Get ready to enjoy a month of glorious spring!

Sewing Kit

This jar gift contains all kinds of sewing and mending supplies complete with a pincushion on top. Here are the items you will need:

> 1-quart widemouthed canning jar with lid
> 6-inch square of fabric
> Fiberfill
> Poster board
> Tape
> Fabric and jewelry glue
> Hot-melt glue (optional)

To make the pincushion, center the ring of the jar on the fabric. Using it as a guide to trace, cut out a circle that is one inch larger than the ring all the way around. Cut out six circles of Fiberfill (stuffing material you can get at craft or fabric stores) that are decreasing in size. The first one should be the size of the jar lid. The second should be a bit smaller and so on until the sixth circle is only 1½ inches across.

From the poster board, cut a circle the size of the jar lid. Pile up the Fiberfill circles on top of the poster board circle. Place the fabric on top. Pick it up like a sandwich and carefully push the fabric and padding up through the underside of the ring and secure it by pushing the poster board over the bottom. Adjust the gathers so the fabric is smooth. Tape the loose ends of the fabric onto the bottom side of the poster board.

Use either fabric glue or hot-melt glue to stick the top side of the lid to the bottom side of the poster board, making sure the fabric edges are all tucked in between the two pieces. Hold securely until the glue cools or sets. If you are using hot glue, be careful because the metal will get very hot. Enough glue should push out from the edges to secure the poster board and fabric to the top under edge of the ring. Allow to set overnight.

Fill the jar with small sewing supplies such as buttons, safety pins, thread, hooks and eyes, scissors, a seam ripper, a tape measure, pins, and needles. Rather than buying all the "ingredients" at once, start watching for sales at craft and fabric stores. You'll be able to fill your jars quite cheaply if you start early. This gift is self-explanatory, so the tag can carry your own personal message.

Play Dough

2 cups	all-purpose flour
1 cup	salt
2 tablespoons	cream of tartar
1 or 2 packages	unsweetened flavored drink mix such as Kool-Aid (optional)

Combine and pour the mixture into the jar. Embellish as desired.

Attach this message to the jar:

–––––– Play Dough ––––––

Pour contents of jar into large microwavable bowl. Add 2 cups water and 2 tablespoons baby oil. Mix well and microwave on high for four minutes, stopping every thirty seconds or so to stir. A ball will form. Cool the dough and store in an airtight container in the refrigerator. Caution: It smells good enough to eat, but please don't.

Candy Cane Bath Salts

12	12-ounce jelly canning jars with lids and rings
8 pounds	Epsom salt, divided
4 pounds (6 cups)	sea salt or kosher salt
½ teaspoon	glycerin, divided (nonedible, drugstore variety)
16 drops	peppermint essential oil, divided
12 to 15 drops	red food coloring

Place 4 pounds Epsom salt into a large mixing bowl. Add 3 cups salt and stir well. Stir in ¼ teaspoon glycerin and 8 drops essential oil. Mix well.

In a second large mixing bowl, place 4 pounds Epsom salt and add 3 cups salt. Stir well. Add ¼ teaspoon glycerin, 8 drops essential oil, and food coloring. Stir until completely blended. Color should be even. Layer bath salts into jars alternating the white and red to create candy cane stripes. Embellish as desired.

Attach this message to the jar:

–––––– Candy Cane Bath Salts ––––––
Add several tablespoons to a warm bath. Enjoy!

Kitchen Potpourri

¼ cup	whole cloves
1 cup	whole allspice
10	cinnamon sticks, each 3 inches long, broken into pieces
8	small bay leaves
4	whole nutmeg
3 tablespoons	star anise
2 tablespoons	cardamom pods

Combine all the ingredients in a bowl, mixing well. Pour into any size decorative jar with a tight-fitting lid.

Attach this message to the jar:

——— Kitchen Potpourri ———

Store indefinitely at room temperature. Remove lid, stirring occasionally to release fragrance, or pour into a small dish.

Bath Oil

½ cup	almond oil
½ cup	castor oil or aloe vera oil or the oil from 6 to 8 vitamin E capsules
25 to 30 drops	fragrance oil

Mix all ingredients in a nonmetal bowl with a wooden spoon until combined. Pour into jar. Embellish as desired.

Attach this message to the jar:

——— Bath Oil ———

Add several drops to a warm bath. Enjoy!

Bubble Bath

3 cups	baby shampoo
	oil from 6 to 8 vitamin E capsules
¼ cup	glycerin
25 to 30 drops	fragrance oil
	Food coloring

Mix all ingredients in a nonmetal bowl with a wooden spoon until combined. Pour into jar. Embellish as desired.

Attach this message to the jar:

——— Bubble Bath ———
Add several drops to a warm bath. Enjoy!

Salt Scrub

Mix together Epsom salt and enough almond oil (better) or baby oil (cheaper) to resemble very wet snow. Add aromatherapy oil of your choice for fragrance and soap colorant if you desire. You can find oils and colorant at craft stores, online at Amazon.com, or at retailers that sell soap and candle-making supplies. Fill small jars and embellish as desired.

Attach this message to the jar:

——— Salt Scrub ———
Scoop out salt mixture and apply to damp skin, using circular movements. Rinse thoroughly to stimulate and exfoliate skin.

Journal in a Jar

A bit more complex than previous jar gifts, a journal in a jar requires the traditional jar plus a gift pack.

The idea is to give everything your recipient needs to write the story of his or her life, including appropriate and specific prompting questions such as: Why was your name chosen for you? What was happening in the world when you were born? What was your favorite hiding place as a child? What is your favorite hiding place as an adult? What is your personal secret to happiness?

You can include as many questions or prompts as you like, even 365 to make it easy for your recipient to pull out one at random each day and write about it.

At first I found this to be a terrific gift idea for a parent or grandparent. But then it dawned on me that this could be adapted for any age, even for a child just learning to read, write, and draw. Prompts can include instructing the child to draw a picture of a favorite animal, place to visit, and so on. For an older child or teen, the prompts can be more detailed, such as asking him or her to describe a favorite pet, band, vacation, or activity.

Attach this message to the jar:

——— Recipe for Your Life History ———

Combine a generous slice of your life history, a dash of nostalgia, several cups of facts and feelings, and [the number you come up with] deliciously interesting questions.

Draw one slip of paper. Take a few minutes to enjoy the memories. Paste or write the question at the top of a blank page. Fill in your answer. Don't worry about your handwriting or spelling—just tell your story.

The purpose of this gift is to help you preserve a written account of your life. Enjoy the homemade memories that celebrate something very important . . . you!

Include with this jar gift a notebook or some writing paper, an appropriate binder, and a nice pen. Include everything required to get started. If your recipient is computer savvy, include an appropriate binder that will fit computer-printed pages.

This is an idea that can be adapted in so many ways. The more you can personalize it, the better. Adapt your questions and prompts to the specific recipient so the result will be more detailed and the answers more complete and specific. Make it fun by including questions you know will make the person laugh because the answers are so hilarious.

To help you get going, you will find a few idea starters below. If you need more, I have posted hundreds for all age groups—as young as 5 and as old as 105—on our website. Just log on to www.debtproofliving.com and click on Mary's Web Desk. You can copy and paste them into your word processing program or write them longhand. Add your own unique questions. Cut them apart and drop them into the jar.

Journal in a jar is not a gift you can make on Christmas Eve. You need to get started now. While you're at it, make one for yourself. It will become a legacy for your children.

Questions for Adults

Why was your name chosen for you?

What was happening in the world when you were born?

What is your earliest memory of home?

What was your favorite hiding place as a child?

What is your favorite hiding place as an adult?

What was your favorite store as a child, and why did you like to go there?

What were your chores?

What did your mother do during the day?

What did you do on summer days?

What did you enjoy in the winter?

What was your favorite fairy tale or bedtime story?

What was your favorite doll or toy?

What was your favorite treat?

What pets have you had?

What pet did you always want?

Do you remember what an ice-cream cone cost when you were a child? What does one cost today?

What kind of car did your family have?

How did people dress when you were a child?

What was your favorite outfit?

How were children expected to behave?

How did you learn about God?

Who set a good example for you?

What was your favorite Scripture passage as a child?

What is your favorite Scripture passage now?

What was your favorite television show as a child or youth?

Describe getting a Christmas tree with your family as a child.

Questions for Older Children

Tell about your favorite pet. When did you get him or her? Why do you like this pet?

What's your favorite thing to do in the summer? Why?

What was your favorite family vacation? Where did you go? What did you see?

What's your favorite movie? Why do you like it? What's it about?

What do you enjoy doing with your grandma or grandpa?

What is the best Christmas present you have received? What is the best one you have given?

What is your favorite thing to play at the park?

If you could have your favorite dinner for your birthday, what would it be?

Who is your favorite friend, and why is he or she special to you?

What are your best and worst subjects in school? What do and don't you like about them?

If you could have any animal as a pet, what kind would you choose and why?

Write something nice your family does that makes you happy.

Tell your favorite joke, or write about something that makes you laugh.

What is your favorite board game or computer game and why do you like it?

If you could watch a movie over and over, what would it be and why? What's it about?

Tell about the house you live in. Have you lived anywhere else? If so, do you remember the addresses, and phone numbers?

Tell about a special birthday party you've had.

How do you like being the oldest, middle, youngest, or only child? Does it have any particular advantages or disadvantages?

Activities for Young Children

Draw a picture of your favorite pet or animal.

Draw a picture of your favorite thing to do in the summer.

Draw a picture of your favorite place to go.

Draw a picture of your favorite thing to do with your grandma or grandpa.

Draw a picture of what you want for Christmas.

Draw a picture of what you play with at the park.

Draw a funny picture about something that makes you laugh.

Draw a picture of the house you live in.

Draw a picture of your favorite birthday present.

Draw a picture of your favorite toy.

Draw a picture of your family.

Draw a picture of anything that you are afraid of.

Draw a picture of what you would buy if you had all the money in the world.

Draw a picture of your favorite outfit to wear.

Draw a picture of your room and what makes it special.

Draw a picture of your favorite holiday using your favorite color.

Christmas has always been a big deal with my family, no matter how short of money we might be. When I could not convince my family to skip gifting for their sake, I decided to opt out of Christmas—a very radical step, met with rolled eyes and raised eyebrows. I told them I was going away and didn't want to participate in any gift exchange. My boyfriend at the time, always thrifty and disciplined, also insisted we not exchange gifts. Gift-giving with a girlfriend always made him nervous. Instead of going away, I secretly made arrangements to work in a local soup kitchen both Christmas Eve and Christmas Day, and my boyfriend and I planned a late-night traditional Italian Christmas Eve dinner. He even gave me his mother's secret recipe for calamari.

Working at the soup kitchen on the 24th was both sobering and inspiring, and I came home ready to prepare our romantic supper, thanking God for being kind enough to do so. When my boyfriend arrived, he asked me repeatedly if I'd cheated and bought him any gifts, but I assured him I had not. Finally, he relaxed.

We had a lovely, peace-filled evening together, and over a particularly decadent dessert I glanced at my Christmas tree and saw two tiny wrapped boxes that did not look familiar. I was puzzled until I saw my boyfriend's pleased expression. He had been convinced he would never have the pleasure of giving me something without receiving something in return. From this man who shied away from gift-giving I received a beautiful pair of pearl earrings and a tiny bottle of my favorite perfume.

The next day at the soup kitchen, as I took up my position behind the drinks station, I realized anew how truly blessed my life was and how much more meaningful Christmas had become when I removed myself from the stress of mass gift-buying and instead chose to spend my time doing something to bring pleasure to others.

I now tailor my gifts to things I can do for people, such as monthly dinners cooked at my parents', memory albums with funny anecdotes, or letters telling the recipient how much he or she means to me. It's a lot more work this way, but it's a gift I give myself as well.

Susan G., Connecticut

"Good grief, Gladys! Why can't you just relax and enjoy the lazy, crazy days of summer like the rest of us?!"

11

Gifts from the Garden

Gardening continues to be a popular hobby, but more than that, it is an excellent way to stretch your food dollars. A homegrown organic tomato costs about a nickel compared to a dollar or more at the market.

If you've ever gardened, you know the challenge of the sudden surplus of one item. What do you do with thirty pounds of tomatoes? Or a carload of zucchini? Think holidays!

Preserving your garden's harvest may be the perfect solution for your holiday gift list. You can bake and freeze zucchini bread and pumpkin bread (wrapped well, loaves freeze well for four months). You can make yummy zucchini relish, spaghetti sauce, salsa, sun-dried tomatoes, applesauce, apple butter, pumpkin seeds, and berry jams. All make excellent gifts.

Here are some of my favorite ways to turn a bountiful season into gifts.

Zucchini Relish

7	zucchinis, unpeeled and chopped
4	large onions, chopped
1	large sweet red bell pepper, chopped
1	4-ounce can chopped green chilies
3 tablespoons	salt
3½ cups	sugar
3 cups	vinegar
1 tablespoon	ground turmeric
4 teaspoons	celery seed
1 teaspoon	black pepper
½ teaspoon	ground nutmeg

In a large container, combine zucchini, onions, red pepper, chilies, and salt. Let rest overnight. The next day, rinse the relish and drain. Place the sugar, vinegar, turmeric, celery seed, pepper, and nutmeg in a large pot over medium-high heat. Bring to a boil. Add relish to the pot and simmer for ten minutes. While it's hot, put into jars. Leave a small space at the top. Fit lids on tightly. Follow proper canning procedures for sealing if relish is to be stored. This does not freeze well.

Salsa

1 tablespoon	olive oil
2	onions, diced
2 cloves	garlic, minced
1	green bell pepper, diced
1	red bell pepper, diced
1	28-ounce can crushed tomatoes OR 2 to 3 cups diced fresh tomatoes
3 teaspoons	wine vinegar
¼ teaspoon	black pepper
1 tablespoon	fresh cilantro, chopped
¼ teaspoon	cayenne pepper or jalapeno peppers to taste

Heat olive oil in a large pot over medium-high heat and sauté onion, garlic, green pepper, and red pepper. Add tomatoes and rest of ingredients to pan and stir. Remove from heat immediately. To preserve, follow proper canning procedures or freeze. Freezer life: one year.

Sun-Dried Tomatoes

6 pounds	ripe tomatoes (preferably Roma variety)
2 tablespoons	salt
3 cups	olive oil

Slice tomatoes lengthwise and arrange on racks or screens. Sprinkle with salt. If drying in the sun, place another screen over the top to keep debris and bugs out. Leave in the sun for eight to twelve hours or bake in a low-heat oven (200°F) until all signs of moisture have disappeared (about eight to nine hours). Remove from oven and allow to cool. Pack in pint-sized jars and cover completely with olive oil. Seal tightly, decorate jars, and refrigerate.

Roasted Pumpkin Seeds

	Seeds from one large or several small pumpkins
2 tablespoons	vegetable oil
1 tablespoon	salt

Clean and rinse the seeds. Spread out on a towel to dry. In a bowl, toss dry seeds with oil and salt. For variety, try a little onion salt or chili powder. Spread the seeds on a cookie sheet. Bake at 350°F for thirty minutes, stirring occasionally. Let cool.

Sweet Pepper Onion Relish

20 to 25	medium-sized sweet red bell peppers, finely chopped
4 to 6	large white sweet onions, finely chopped
3 to 4	very finely chopped jalapeno peppers (or more depending on your desire for heat)
3½ cups	white sugar
3 cups	apple cider vinegar
2 tablespoons	salt

Place all ingredients in a large pot. Stir to blend thoroughly. Bring to a low boil. Reduce heat and simmer for thirty to forty minutes, until the vegetables are soft and glistening and the liquid has thickened. Spoon into jars, apply the lids while the relish is still hot, allow to cool, and store in the refrigerator.

Pour over cream cheese and serve with crackers, place alongside beef or poultry, or eat (shhhh!) straight from the jar.

Pesto a la Genovese

Whether grown in your garden or in a container—or purchased at a produce stand—basil is the main ingredient in this gourmet food item that is sure to please just about everyone on your gift list this holiday season.

1½ cups	fresh basil leaves, packed
½ teaspoon	salt
¼ teaspoon	ground black pepper
¼ cup	grated Parmesan cheese
2 tablespoons	pine nuts, toasted
1 teaspoon	minced garlic
½ cup	extra-virgin olive oil

Place pine nuts in a small skillet and heat over medium heat until they begin to turn golden. In the bowl of a food processor (or blender), combine the basil, salt, and pepper and process for a few seconds until the basil is chopped. Add the cheese, pine nuts, and garlic. While the processor is running, add the oil in a thin, steady stream until a mostly smooth sauce is formed.

Notes:

1. If you do not have a food processor, you can make this recipe in a blender using the purée setting.
2. This recipe multiplies well, but do not try to make more than a double batch in a blender or triple in a food processor.
3. Make sure your tools, equipment, and hands are impeccably clean. The introduction of any bacteria may cause the pesto to turn dark.
4. Pesto may be made several days in advance and kept refrigerated in an airtight container until ready to use. If making in advance, be sure to cover the top of the pesto with a thin layer of olive oil to prevent the pesto from darkening. Pesto may also be frozen in the same manner in small quantities for use at a later date.
5. Keep frozen at 0°F or below. Frozen shelf life is one year. When thawed and kept refrigerated at 40°F, product has a shelf life of ten days.
6. For gifts, pour the pesto into small glass jars with lids and rims and place them in the freezer, making sure to leave about ½ inch head room for expansion.

Attach this message to the jar:

——— Pesto a la Genovese ———

This all-natural pesto was made in the Genovese style with fresh basil, olive oil, garlic, pine nuts, and Parmesan cheese. To use, toss with hot pasta, use as a crostini topping, or use as a marinade for chicken or fish. Keep refrigerated and use within one week. Enjoy!

Freezer Strawberry Jam

2 cups	crushed fresh strawberries
4 cups	sugar
1	(1.75-ounce) package dry fruit pectin (do not substitute liquid fruit pectin)
¾ cup	water

Mix crushed strawberries with sugar and let stand for ten minutes. Meanwhile, stir the pectin into the water in a small saucepan. Bring to a boil over medium-high heat and boil for one minute. Stir the boiling water into the strawberries. Allow to stand for three minutes before pouring into jars or other storage containers. Place tops on the containers and leave for twenty-four hours. Place in freezer and store frozen until ready to use.

This jam can remain frozen for up to one year without losing any of its summer-fresh goodness. Once thawed, it should be consumed within three weeks and should be kept refrigerated.

When giving as a gift, add this tag:

—— Strawberry Jam ——

This homemade jam will be best when consumed within three weeks. Do not allow to remain at room temperature; must be kept refrigerated.

Freezer Berry Jam

4 cups	fresh blueberries
2 cups	fresh raspberries
5 cups	sugar
2 tablespoons	lemon juice
¾ cup	water
1	(1.75-ounce) package dry fruit pectin (do not substitute liquid fruit pectin)

In a large bowl, crush the blueberries. Add raspberries and crush. Stir in sugar and lemon juice. Let stand for ten minutes. In a small saucepan, bring water and pectin to a boil. Boil for one minute, stirring constantly.

Add to fruit mixture and stir for three minutes. Pour into jars or freezer containers; cool to room temperature, about thirty minutes. Cover and let stand overnight or until set but not longer than twenty-four hours. Freeze for up to one year.

When giving as a gift, add this tag:

—— Berry Jam ——

This homemade jam will be best when consumed within three weeks. Do not allow to remain at room temperature; must be kept refrigerated.

Refrigerator Pickles

1 cup	distilled white vinegar
1 tablespoon	salt
2 cups	white sugar
6 cups	sliced cucumbers
1 cup	sliced onions
1 cup	sliced green bell peppers

In a medium saucepan over medium heat, bring vinegar, salt, and sugar to a boil. Boil until the sugar has dissolved, about ten minutes.

Place the cucumbers, onions, and green bell peppers in a large bowl. Pour the vinegar mixture over the vegetables. Transfer to sterile containers and store in the refrigerator for up to six months.

Bread and Butter Pickles

25	cucumbers, thinly sliced
6	onions, thinly sliced
2	green bell peppers, diced
3 cloves	garlic, chopped
½ cup	salt
3 cups	cider vinegar
5 cups	white sugar
2 tablespoons	mustard seed
1½ teaspoons	celery seed
½ teaspoon	whole cloves
1 tablespoon	ground turmeric

In a large bowl, mix together cucumbers, onions, green bell peppers, garlic, and salt. Allow to stand approximately three hours. In a large saucepan, mix the cider vinegar, sugar, mustard seed, celery seed, whole cloves, and turmeric. Bring to a boil.

Drain liquid from the cucumber mixture. Stir the cucumber mixture into the boiling vinegar mixture. Remove from heat shortly before the combined mixtures return to a boil. Transfer to sterile containers. Seal and store in the refrigerator up to six months.

Drying Plant Material

Purchasing dried flowers during the holidays can be very expensive. But during the year if you pick wildflowers, receive gifts of flowers, or make cuttings from your own yard, if handled properly, you will have all kinds of wonderful material for holiday projects. If every season you are on the lookout for ways you can recycle nature's bounty, you will have wonderful decorations for Christmas packages, wreaths, garlands, and centerpieces.

Designate a place in your home where you can gather and store dried material. I have a large box in a closet, which I can get to easily and where everything stays dry.

In principle, all plant material can be dried. Selecting the proper method is the key.

Drying by pressing. Flowers that are delicate, with thin petals and leaves, can be dried between sheets of absorbent paper inserted between the pages of a thick book. In two or three weeks, the book's weight presses out the flowers' moisture. A ribbon, bow, and pressed flower adorning a gift wrapped in brown kraft paper make a very elegant package.

Drying by hanging. Flowers such as roses, hydrangea, yarrow, baby's breath, heather, statice, and larkspur can be air-dried simply by tying them in bunches and hanging them upside down in a dark, cool, dry place where air can circulate around them.

Herbs that dry well this way include English pennyroyal, lavender, wild thyme, and rosemary. Simply divide the herbs into small bunches, hang them in a well-ventilated spot, and allow them to dry for about ten days. Gently wrap them in tissue paper and put them away until December. If you aren't up to growing your own herbs, buy them in season at farmer's markets, grocery stores, and gourmet shops.

Drying by desiccants. Desiccants are moisture-absorbing substances such as sand, silica gel, borax, and yellow cornmeal. Silica gel, available at garden shops, drugstores, craft shops, and floral supply stores, is by far the best because it is lightweight, won't damage the flowers, and can be used over and over again. (Silica gel isn't really a gel at all. It resembles granulated sugar.) With silica gel, the drying process generally takes one to two weeks, compared to three weeks or more with sand.

Fill a jar halfway with silica gel. Gently insert a piece of florist wire into each flower. Stand the flower upright in the jar and gently pour in enough crystals to cover all the petals. Seal the container for at least two weeks.

Drying in the microwave. The latest and fastest way to dry flowers is the microwave method. You'll need a microwavable container or cardboard box with a tight-fitting lid. Layer about one inch of silica gel in the bottom of the container. Place the flowers or leaves on top of this layer, leaving about an inch between the container's side and the individual flowers. Add another one-inch layer of silica gel on top.

Place your uncovered container in the microwave. If you're using a cardboard box, elevate it on a microwavable drain rack so the moisture can escape through the bottom of the box.

If your microwave has settings from 2 to 10, put it on setting 4 (about 300 watts); a microwave with three or four settings should be put on half (about 350 watts); and a microwave with high and defrost settings should be set on defrost (about 200 watts). Because microwave ovens vary, you'll need to experiment with the "cooking" times. The drying time for one to five flowers with leaves in about a half pound of silica gel is roughly two to two and a half minutes.

Remove the container from the microwave, cover the container tightly, and allow it to stand for up to thirty minutes. Then empty the container onto a newspaper and gently remove the flowers.

Reusing silica gel. This stuff is so cool. When totally dry, it is blue. As the granules start to absorb moisture, they turn whitish-pink. So just keep checking the color, and when you know they've reached full capacity, you can turn them back to blue. Preheat your conventional oven to 300°F. Spread a single layer of silica gel evenly on the bottom of a shallow pan and place it uncovered in the oven. Stir the granules every once in a while and watch them turn blue. Allow to cool and immediately place the silica gel into an airtight container.

One year my husband and I were on active duty and living with our four-year-old son in Frankfurt, Germany. For our son, Pat, Christmas in Germany was a magical experience, and I went all out to make our holidays as European as I could. I'd planned a special German meal, which we would enjoy before we sang carols, told stories, and opened our gifts.

On that Christmas Eve, we were blessed with a beautiful snowfall—the stage was set. Then, at about 8 p.m., the power went out. Without electricity, I could not cook, we had no beautifully lit tree, and our apartment was dark. I was crushed. With flashlight in hand, my husband gently told me that our son had a solution.

With childlike inquisitiveness, Pat asked if I had any green veg-etables (lettuce), red vegetables (tomatoes), and cheese. I did. He discovered taco shells in our little pantry, and he and my husband went to work. That night we lit candles around our tree, sang carols, told stories, and we shared our first Christmas tacos, which, my son explained, had special meaning: Round taco shells represented a Christmas wreath, decorated with lettuce greenery and red tomato ornaments and sprinkled with grated cheese that looked like lights. We savored this special meal like none other.

Every year since that Christmas in Germany, for going on twenty years, we turn off all the house lights, gather around a candlelit tree, sing songs, and share memories, including the story of Pat's Christmas tacos, which, by the way, taste just as good as they did in Germany.

Dianna P., email

12

Family Gifts

Whether your family tree is a small sapling or a mighty oak, chances are you would like to give gifts to everyone in your extended family. But the cost of buying or making individual gifts for everyone on your list can be daunting. The solution for you this year could be a family gift—a calendar, a cookbook, a family publication, or even a gift basket that is unique to your extended family. Once you make the first gift, you can simply reproduce it to make the same for every family in your family tree.

After you see the potential and read about these gift projects, you are likely to come up with ideas of your own. Don't delay. Projects such as these typically require more time than money.

Family Calendar

The first one I ever saw completely blew me away. An artistically talented young mother drew, lettered, and illustrated by hand a calendar for the coming year in the typical one-month-per-page format. Each month also featured an original drawing depicting a family event that was seasonally appropriate for that particular month.

Next, she hand lettered every possible special occasion and remembrance that would be meaningful for both her immediate and extended families in the coming year: birthdays, anniversaries, vacations, and holidays. She included whimsical events such as National Opening Day of Little League Season and Last Day of School. She illustrated all of these special occasions on the appropriate date. Each month was a visual burst of anticipation and joy.

The talented woman made color photocopies, bound each calendar with ribbon, and gave them as Christmas gifts. Because color photocopiers do such a great job, it was impossible for me to tell the original from the copies.

She gave one of these calendars to each family in her rather large extended family. What a treasure!

You can start with this idea to create your own unique family calendar. It's a gift that will be used throughout the year and then cherished as a family keepsake.

Thankfully, you do not have to be an artist. You can start with a blank calendar from the office supply store and embellish it with photographs and data. You can create yours on a computer. If you have a scanner, digital camera, and printer, you can take the family calendar idea to new heights.

Possibly the most important ingredient in this project is time. Unless you keep very good records, you will have to do some research. And that's just fine, because you've got time.

You will be the hero of your family if you are careful to include every person's name and date of birth, including the year, the full date of wedding anniversaries, and other memorable events.

For older family members who find it particularly challenging to send greeting cards and to remember so many birthdays and special occasions throughout the year, you might consider adding a pocket page at the back of their calendar. Fill it with greeting cards appropriate for each of the year's special occasions. Include the mailing addresses and tuck in a sheet of postage stamps too. You'll be remembered fondly nearly every day of the year as you help them to keep in touch.

Epson, Hewlett Packard, and Microsoft all offer templates for you to download. Go to their websites and look for services for home computers, crafts, seasonal downloads, etc. You can insert photographs, edit data for special days, and then print out each page. The binding is up to you.

If you'd rather hire someone to do a lot of the work, go to FedEx Kinko's website (Kinkos.com will still take you there) to create your calendar online (look for "Cards and Calendars"). It will cost around twenty dollars depending on what you select. Wait a few days for the finished product to arrive in the mail. Now you have a master calendar onto which you can write important data by hand and embellish to make it unique to your family. Once complete, take the binding apart, and you can make as many colored photocopies as you need. Other websites to check are Ofoto.com and Shutterfly.com.

No computer? No artistic talent? No scanner or digital camera? No problem. You can go into an office supply shop such as Kinko's, hand the clerk twelve photographs, identify which month each one is for, pay about $24.95 for a photo calendar, and come back in a day to pick it up. Now you can customize and embellish with stickers and markers to make it your special family calendar.

One final word of caution: If you do this too well, you unwittingly may establish a new family tradition. And you know what that means? Your family will eagerly anticipate a new edition of your family calendar every year.

That may not be such a bad idea.

Family Cookbook

One of the best ways to tie a ribbon of love around your family tree is to create a family cookbook. I don't know what it is about food, but it touches the soul. It has a way of gluing families together. Perhaps this is the year you should consider putting together a family cookbook. I can't think of a more amazing gift to give all the members of your family than to organize and publish a family cookbook.

Recording a family's recipes preserves an important piece of your heritage to pass on from one generation to the next. But before you make a quick decision to publish your family's cookbook this year, you need to know that this is a serious project. Depending on the size and scope of your design, it could be challenging. So think this through carefully. While handwriting an entire cookbook is a possibility, it's not practical. This is a project for a computer.

Will you do this together with several other family members or go it alone? If others are willing to pitch in, you'll make easy work of this large task. However, it is a project that one person can do quite efficiently.

Design. Before you start, you need to outline what your cookbook will entail. Of course, you'll have recipes, but will you also include biographical information about family members? Stories or anecdotes that tie these recipes to your family? Pictures? Clip art? What size will you make your final cookbook? Will you bind the pages together? Will you make photocopies or print it yourself?

Collection. Write a simple letter to all of your family members requesting that they send you recipes according to the criteria you've chosen. Be sure to give a deadline or you'll be collecting recipes on Christmas Eve. It is important to include current recipes being used by family members too. Remember, all of you are creating history as you live your lives. Remind your family members to double-check the ingredients and the measurements.

Compilation. And now the fun begins. You can build your cookbook using a word processing program such as Microsoft Word, which offers a variety of useful templates. If you are experienced in Word, you'll do well. My experience is that Word is not as friendly as I'd like. This is why I suggest that you seriously consider investing in software specifically designed for creating a family cookbook. Take a look at CookbookWizard.com. For less than thirty dollars, you will make your life considerably easier while turning out a visually pleasing gift that is easy to read, uniform in style, and very useful.

Other additions. Consider leaving room to include your family tree, favorite stories about family members, a history of where the family came from, as well as photos. Everyone loves the photos! Add some quirky interest with trivia you'll find at the "On this day in history . . ." website (History.com/tdih.do).

Binding. Once you've printed the pages for your cookbook, it's time to put them together. Your method of binding will be determined greatly by how many pages you end up with. If you want the cookbook to open flat, use comb binding. This is a plastic spine similar to spiral binding. Copy shops offer this type of binding for a reasonable price.

If it is a fairly thin booklet, you can punch holes through the pages and string twine or ribbon through the holes to hold the pages securely. Or a local print or office supply store such as OfficeMax or Kinko's will be happy to do the printing, copying, and binding for you, though your choices of bindings there will be limited.

Family Christmas Letter

If you can compose a decent sentence and have access to a few modern-day tools, you have all you need to create a unique and priceless gift—a family Christmas letter. Done well, it will be treasured by those who receive it, and that's a gift money cannot buy.

Content. Tell about the past year using character sketches of family members. Entertain your readers with anecdotes that show rather than describe just how brilliant and clever your family members are. Good quotes, especially from little ones' backseat conversations, are like pure gold. Interview your kids to come up with great material.

Appearance. If your letter doesn't immediately captivate your reader, the best content in the world will go straight into the trash can. The care you take in the letter's appearance shows the respect you have for your reader.

Length. Keep it to two pages, three at the most. There's beauty in simplicity. Don't do as one woman who sent me her twenty-eight-page, two-sided, single-spaced account of every single day of the entire year. Your goal is to leave your readers wishing for more, not pleading for less.

White space. This is the area on a page that is not covered by print. If you are conscious of big blank white spaces, you have too much white space. If you squint your eyes and the entire page looks gray, you don't have enough. A judicious use of white space gives your readers' eyes a chance to rest.

Margins. This is mandatory white space. One and a half inches at the top and at least one inch at the bottom, right, and left are good rules of thumb.

Fonts. Control yourself. Even though you have 579 choices readily available, use no more than three in the same letter. Two is better.

Punctuation. There are specific rules about everything from quotation mark placement to spaces between sentences. When you care enough to punctuate correctly, you show respect for your readers' intelligence. Visit TeacherVision.com and type "proper punctuation" in the search box.

Pictures. You can increase your letter's value by including special photos. Make sure your pictures do not collide with your text. Be sure to allow for buffer space—a margin of at least ¼ inch between the edges of the picture and where the text begins. When it comes to photos and clip art, more is tacky, less is lovely.

Proofreading. It's difficult to find your own errors, and spell-checkers are not completely reliable. Ask a couple of people to proofread your final version.

Simplicity. When you have a choice between a long word and a short word, go with the short one. Strip every sentence so all that remains are the cleanest components. Examine every word and keep only those that are necessary. Don't say "At this point in time" when you can say "Now."

Etiquette. The purpose of your family letter is to reacquaint readers with your family and to convey your wishes for their joyful holiday. Keep to these rules:

1. No press releases. This is not the right time to review your amazing career and most recent promotion.
2. No fund-raising. You do have a captive audience, but curb the urge to ask for donations for your next mission trip or sponsors for your kids' Jog-a-Thon.
3. No sales pitches. It is not cool to include an invitation to your next Tupperware party or mention that you have an amazing business opportunity to share.

Start now. Letters thrown together at the last minute usually show it.

Gift Baskets

A basket filled with delicious treats and fun gadgets will please just about anyone on your gift list if it's tailor-made. Choose an attractive container—it doesn't have to be a basket—decorate and fill it. Your "basket" can be as simple or as extravagant, as big or as small, as your budget and imagination allow.

A gift basket is a great gift for an entire family, including the pets. The basket itself can actually cost less than fancy wrapping paper. No matter what time of year it is right now, start looking for elegant but cheap baskets and containers. A great source for beautiful yet inexpensive baskets is stores such as Trader Joe's, Big Lots, and World Market.

Once you start thinking creatively, you won't have to worry about where to shop to start filling your baskets but rather when to stop. As you fill the basket, lean items at an angle rather than stacking everything vertically. Presentation is most important.

Family fun night. Fill a large bowl or other container with everything required: DVDs, microwave popcorn, theater-sized boxes of candy, a puzzle, a deck of cards, and bottles of soda.

Party of two. Include boxes of dry pasta, a jar of spaghetti sauce (homemade would be nice), breadsticks, candlesticks, and a CD of classical Italian music.

Christmas in a box. For someone living alone, send a tabletop tree, a string of garland, a tree topper, lights, and a box of ornaments. Also include a CD of Christmas carols to be played while decorating the tree.

Bookworm basket. Fill a basket with a few books; a coffee mug; packets of hot chocolate, instant coffee, or tea; a tin of cookies; and a pillow.

Letter writer's basket. Include assorted greeting cards, postcards, stationery, postage stamps, pens, pencils, and return address labels.

Gift wrap basket. Include curling ribbon, wrapping paper, gift cards, transparent tape, scissors, gift bags, and tissue paper.

Bath basket. Fill a basket with bubble bath, lotion, bath powder, fragrance, scented candles, a back brush, a loofah sponge, soap, a book, and a CD of relaxing music.

Gourmet's basket. Include fresh dried herbs tied in a bundle, fresh spices, unique kitchen tools, recipe cards, and jars of gourmet mustards and salsas.

Artist's basket. Include brushes, brush cleaner, a sketch pad, a palette, a beret, sponges, a small canvas, and colored pencils.

Picnic basket. Fill a basket with a tablecloth, napkins, plastic plates, utensils, candleholders, candles, salt and pepper shakers, plastic bags, and bug spray.

Mother of a preschooler basket. Include activity books and games for the kids, coping manuals, babysitting coupons for a night or weekend away from it all, bubble bath, and a romantic novel.

Pizza basket. Fill a basket with checkered napkins, a pizza stone, recipes, special flour, spices, a jar of pizza sauce, cheese, and a pizza cutter.

Gardener's basket. Fill a basket with work gloves, a trowel, seed-marking stakes, seeds or bulbs, decorative pots, a sun bonnet, a tiny birdhouse, and sunscreen.

Breakfast in a basket. Include homemade jelly, pancake mix, muffin mix, a biscuit cutter, honey, cinnamon sugar, mugs, gourmet coffee, a crêpe pan, favorite recipes, and tea.

Coffee lover's basket. Include a bag of exotic coffee beans, a coffee mug, bagels, and a bagel cutter.

When our girls were small, they got caught up in the "I wants" of Christmas, so we started a new tradition. Every Christmas we would set aside a certain amount of money, and we and the girls would spend the weeks before Christmas looking and praying for people who might have a need we could meet. The catch was that we had to get the money or gift to them without them knowing who gave it. That way they could only thank God. If we got caught, we put more money in the fund and tried again. The girls absolutely loved it, and it changed their thinking from what they could get to what they could give.

P.B., email

One year my oldest daughter from New Hampshire could not get up to Pittsfield, Maine, for either Thanksgiving or Christmas, so she started a new tradition. It was a celebration between the two holidays on a weekend when we could all manage to get together. She began calling it Thanksmas. We have a meal, exchange gifts, and thank God for each other. We alternate holding the event at her house and ours.

Elizabeth C., email

13

Traditions Are the Glue That Holds Us Together

Does anyone remember the marginally entertaining TV show *Supermarket Sweep*? Contestants had several minutes to fill grocery carts with as much stuff as possible. The winner wasn't determined by the quantity of stuff jammed into the cart but by the total monetary value at checkout. The contestant with the biggest tab won the game.

The strategy was simple. Pass up the low-value stuff and load up on what's going to pay off big at the checkout. Smart contestants had a plan of action and knew exactly where to head the minute the clock started ticking.

Christmas is like that. Once the season begins, you'll start filling your shopping cart. You'll have lots of choices. What you choose will either pay off in terms of happiness, satisfaction, and pleasant holiday memories, or you'll get negative results of dissatisfaction and disappointment fueled by guilt, obligation, and trying to meet others' expectations. What you end up with when it's all put away for another year will depend on the choices you make between now and then.

Measuring Holiday Value

In their book *Unplug the Christmas Machine*, authors Jo Robinson and Jean C. Staeheli say that while children may be quick to tell their parents they want designer clothes, the latest electronic gear, and name-brand toys for Christmas, underneath, here's what they really want:[9]

relaxed and loving time with family

realistic expectations about gifts

an evenly paced holiday season

reliable family traditions

Underneath, I think that's what adults want too.

Just imagine how the holidays might look this year if we have the courage to hold each of our choices and holiday decisions against the measuring stick of the four things we really want for Christmas.

Relaxed and Loving Time with Family

If you're looking for a big payoff in terms of happiness this holiday season, this is where you want to concentrate your efforts. That's because experts tell us that happiness is the process of enjoying what we're doing. Happiness is found in our relationships, our free time, our family, and our lives.

The secret here is to schedule blocks of family time in the same way you would an important meeting with a client or lunch with a friend. Write them on the calendar. Do it now and do it in ink. It's that important.

Idea: Fill shoeboxes for Operation Christmas Child, an organization that distributes gifts to children in desperate situations around the world. For specific information on how to get involved, go to Samaritans Purse.org.

Idea: Spend time alone with each of your children, putting together puzzles, making gifts, decorating the tree, baking, shopping, laughing, reading, or even playing video games.

Idea: Have someone in the family log on to FamilyFun.com and find a Christmas craft that uses only stuff you already have around the house. You won't believe all the ideas you will discover.

Idea: Call a local nursing home and ask a staff member for the names of several residents who rarely have visitors or receive mail. "Adopt" them for the holidays by sending a Christmas card or paying a personal visit. Take the kids. Let them experience the joy of giving to others.

Realistic Expectations about Gifts

No one can determine what having realistic expectations about gifts means for your specific situation. But it's safe to say that if your gift plan requires you to go into debt, it's not realistic. If it means sixty gifts per child, it's not realistic. If it means feeling obligated to exchange gifts with each member of your extended family, that too may be unrealistic for you this year.

Now is the right time to decide what is right for you and your family. Set boundaries when it comes to both giving and receiving gifts. Realistic gifts for you may be simple, handmade gifts from your kitchen.

Even if you're not particularly crafty, you can assemble wonderful consumable gifts that will not clutter others' lives with more stuff. Jar gifts are a great idea (see chapter 10).

Idea: No new gifts. The idea is that you can only give something you already have that another person would enjoy as well.

Idea: If you have very young children, arrange with other families to swap toys instead of everyone buying new ones this year. Clean them up, wrap them up, and the kids will be none the wiser.

Idea: Some families include service to others as part of their holiday gift-giving. Make coupon books that family members can redeem for services such as car washing, making a favorite meal, or cleaning the garage. Physical labor never goes out of style.

An Evenly Paced Holiday Season

I know this is probably the last thing you want to hear right now, but it's true: You've got to get organized. No matter how simple or complex your holidays, organization is the only way to keep things evenly paced.

Idea: The website OrganizedChristmas.com is the next best thing to hiring a professional organizer. It'll put you in the mood for Christmas and actually make you think getting organized is great fun.

Idea: Make meals ahead and freeze them. On those very busy days in mid-December, you'll stay relaxed and stress-free knowing that dinner will be on the table as usual. Your family is used to that, right?

Idea: This idea is so useful it bears repeating. Get one envelope for each person on your gift list. Write that person's name and the amount you plan to spend on the front. Put the cash in the envelope. When you go shopping, take the envelopes—not your checkbook or plastic. When an envelope is empty, stop shopping.

Reliable Family Traditions

Traditions give families assurance that even in an uncertain and changing world there are some things they can count on to be the same. Anything you do in the same way at the same time, year after year, counts as a tradition.

Make a list of your family's best traditions. Talk about them, treat them with a sense of respect and joy, and add to them. Repeat them often, and in time they will become trusted anchors in your lives.

Idea: Honor your family's heritage by teaching your kids how to make the foods of that country or region. Learn the songs and customs of that culture.

Idea: As Christmas draws near, go out into your community to look at Christmas lights. Everyone gets ready for bed (pjs on, teeth brushed), then the entire family piles into the car. Take blankets along to add coziness. Choose your favorite house—everyone in the family gets a vote. If you're especially ambitious, drop off a Christmas card to thank them for brightening your holiday season.

Idea: When no one is looking, Santa's elves string Christmas lights in the kids' rooms. No matter how many times you do this, it will still be the best surprise.

Idea: There is a way you can give your kids what they really want this year. And in doing this, you will establish a new family tradition they'll want to repeat year after year:

1. Between now and December, collect twenty-four books that are in keeping with your family's values and beliefs for the holidays.
2. Wrap each book as a beautiful gift, then place all twenty-four in a large basket or festively decorated box. Keep the box hidden until December 1. If you want to avoid potential arguments when you get to step 3, number each gift 1 through 24 to correspond to the days of the month.
3. Each night before bed, allow the children to select and open one of the gifts, or follow the numbers you've placed on the packages, and then read it together. Repeat each night through Christmas Eve.
4. Put the books away in a secret place and you'll be ready to go again next year—and every year—starting with step 2.

What makes this an excellent tradition is that it is enjoyed over a three- to four-week period. The kids do not spend months waiting for a celebration that is over in a few hours of frenzied gift unwrapping. And it fulfills the need in all of us for an evenly paced holiday season.

There are three basic types of Christmas books for children: books about the nativity—some based on the Bible, others on legends; books about Santa Claus, gift-giving, and the like; and books that relate to one or more of the above but don't quite fit into any category. To decide what books you want, it's best to take the time to read through books that interest you or to read reviews.

Don't have money available to invest in books? Perhaps you can borrow from friends or relatives. Or put together your list at your public library, then make your reservations early so you can pick them up right after Thanksgiving. Make sure you know your library's renewal policy. Many libraries will renew books by phone or online.

With months to plan, you have a world of possibilities for locating just the right books for your family. Search garage sales, used bookstores, and other resources. New Christmas books are available in retail bookstores everywhere starting in early November, but you will have a window of opportunity of only about four to eight weeks. However, you can shop anytime of year at sites that offer quality used books such as Half.com and Amazon.com. I located many of the books that follow at these sites for less than a buck each, plus shipping and handling.

While this project is perfect for families, it can be easily adapted by grandparents, teachers, libraries, and Sunday school classes too. No children in your life? This is a project you could put together and then send to a family in a faraway place that would not otherwise be able to celebrate Christmas every day during December.

To help you get started with this project—and to weed through the vast number of Christmas books for children—I asked our online members to nominate their favorite children's Christmas books. We narrowed the field to this list of twenty-four books, including one for Hanukkah:

1. *The Story of Holly and Ivy*, by Rumer Godden (Puffin, 32 pages, ISBN 9780142416839). Orphaned Ivy finds her Christmas wish fulfilled with the help of a lonely couple and a doll named Holly.
2. *The Best Christmas Present of All*, by Linda Jennings (Puffin, 32 pages, ISBN 9780140566468). After his elderly owner suffers a heart attack, Buster the dog is sent to live with the man's grandchildren and in the confusion tries to return home.
3. *Peef: The Christmas Bear*, by Tom Hegg (Waldman House Press, 48 pages, ISBN 9780931674266). A Christmas teddy bear made by Santa comes to life and yearns to belong and bring happiness to one small child.
4. *Room for a Little One*, by Martin Waddell (Margaret K. McElderry, 32 pages, ISBN 9781416925187). 'Tis the eve of Christmas—a cold winter's night—when Kind Ox offers to share his stable by the inn.
5. *The Other Wise Man*, retold by Pamela Kennedy (Ideals Publications, 32 pages, ISBN 9780824953485). The story of the fourth wise man and his search for the Christ child.
6. *The Tale of Three Trees*, by Angela Elwell Hunt (Cook Communications, 25 pages, ISBN 9780745917436). Three trees dream of what they want to become when they grow up. Their dreams come true in the most unexpected of ways as one becomes the

manger, another Christ's boat, and the third the cross upon which he was crucified.

7. *The Christmas Child*, by Max Lucado (Thomas Nelson, 48 pages, ISBN 9780849917684). This Christmas treasure, formerly titled *The Christmas Cross*, features the story of a Chicago journalist who discovers the meaning of Christmas.

8. *The Christmas Miracle of Jonathan Toomey*, by Susan Wojciechowski (Candlewick, 40 pages, ISBN 9780763636296). A tender, elegant, and poignant story about the spiritual re-awakening of a bitter man.

9. *The Best Christmas Pageant Ever*, by Barbara Robinson (Harper Collins, 128 pages, ISBN 9780064402750). A hilarious and touching story about the transformation of the Herdmans, the worst kids in the history of the world. Christmas becomes new and real in some pretty surprising ways.

10. *Eight Nights of Hanukkah*, by Michael J. Rosen (Scholastic, 32 pages, ISBN 9780439365741). A story written from a child's perspective about how one particular family celebrates Hanukkah.

11. *The Polar Express*, by Chris Van Allsburg (Houghton Mifflin, 32 pages, ISBN 9780395389492). A little boy who still believes in Santa takes a magical train ride on Christmas Eve to the North Pole.

12. *Merry Christmas Mom and Dad*, by Mercer Mayer (Random House, 24 pages, ISBN 9780307118868). Trying to be good for Christmas without bungling everything is difficult for this little one.

13. *A Pussycat's Christmas*, by Margaret Wise Brown (Katherine Tegen Books, 32 pages, ISBN 9780061869785). A Pussycat Christmas is made up of sights and sounds that capture the mystery and beauty of the holiday.

14. *The Littlest Christmas Tree*, by Janie Jasin (Book Peddlers, 32 pages, ISBN 9780916773816). The smallest seedling on the tree farm dreams about the things she could become and realizes becoming a Christmas tree is one of the many options.

15. *The Berenstain Bears Meet Santa Bear*, by Stan and Jan Berenstain (Random House, 32 pages, ISBN 9780679805939). Sister

Bear enjoys Christmas preparations, especially getting her list ready. But on Christmas morning she realizes what Christmas is really all about.

16. *Nutcracker*, by E. T. A. Hoffman (Crown, 120 pages, ISBN 9780609610497). An engaging treatment of a classic story that is not just a Christmas story but a wonderful parable for every season.

17. *Morris' Disappearing Bag*, by Rosemary Wells (Puffin, 40 pages, ISBN 9780142300046). It's Christmas Day, and Morris is missing. This warm and humorous story proves that sometimes the littlest bunny gets the last laugh.

18. *How the Grinch Stole Christmas!* by Dr. Seuss (Random House, 64 pages, ISBN 9780394800790). The Grinch, whose heart is two sizes too small, hates Who-ville's holiday celebrations and plans to steal all the presents to prevent Christmas from coming. To his amazement, Christmas comes anyway.

19. *Max's Christmas*, by Rosemary Wells (Viking Juvenile, 32 pages, ISBN 9780670887156). Max, the irrepressible bunny, sneaks downstairs to wait for Santa, with unexpected results!

20. *Red Ranger Came Calling*, by Berkeley Breathed (Little, Brown, 32 pages, ISBN 9780316102490). A cynical young man, the Red Ranger of Mars, meets his match in a retired Santa.

21. *A Christmas Carol*, by Charles Dickens (Sterling, 96 pages, ISBN 9781402766909). Probably one of the most beloved Christmas stories in history, this has it all: heroes, villains, ghosts, time travel, long-lost love, and a happy ending. You may want to opt for a condensed version of the full-length book.

22. *Littlest Angel*, by Charles Tazewell (Ideals, 32 pages, ISBN 978 0824955755). Adapted from the 1946 original about a cherub and his present to the Son of God.

23. *A Charlie Brown Christmas*, by Charles M. Schulz (Simon & Schuster, 32 pages, ISBN 9781416913795). Everyone is getting into the Christmas spirit—except for Charlie Brown. It seems everybody has forgotten what Christmas is truly about.

24. *The Night Before Christmas*, by Clement Clarke Moore (Putnam, 32 pages, ISBN 9780399231902). One of the many variations of the classic story, with delightful illustrations by Jan Brett.

New Family Traditions

Every year in the weeks leading up to the holidays, I get a number of letters from readers asking for help with starting new family traditions.

One year recently I decided to poll the entire membership of Debt-Proof Living online, asking readers to send in their best traditions to share with others.

It wasn't easy selecting some of the responses to share with you in the limited space I have here. Some were moving, others quite hilarious. So whether you're looking for ideas for your family or you are curious to know how others observe Christmas, here for your pre-holiday enjoyment is a selection of favorite family traditions:

 Each year we buy a new jigsaw puzzle and start it at the kitchen table. It provides a spot for one or more family members or visitors to sit, visit, and take a few minutes to relax and work on the puzzle together. We've had some good conversations while working on puzzles! We try to finish it before the Christmas festivities begin, but it doesn't always work out that way.

 I know Christmas is supposed to be a time of love and harmony and family. But after many years of putting up with the stress of our bickering relatives, my husband and I made our own tradition. We travel every year from December 20 to 27. Just the two of us. That's our gift to each other. Our best trip was on Amtrak across the South. Next we plan to go across Canada. We arrive home relaxed and happy instead of stressed-out and angry.

 Years ago we began taking pictures of all the grandchildren in front of my mom's Christmas tree. The first year the picture was a surprise gift for her. Now, many years later, we're still taking the same pose with a few new grandchildren added along the way. We make reprints for all the siblings, so we all have pictures from each Christmas. It's great to see how the kids have grown from year to year. My mom has them framed and all arranged in order in the hallway. It is wonderful.

 Here's a fun one my dad has been doing for years. He got tired of the fact that he never knew what was in all the packages to us that were signed from "him" and my mother. One year he got a large black trash bag for each of his daughters, their husbands and kids, and my mother. Starting in January, he began putting stuff in the bags: rolls of quarters, clothes with his company logo, trinkets that people were peddling at his office during the year—anything and everything. Now one of the highlights for all of us on Christmas Day is "opening the trash bags." You never know what will be in there!

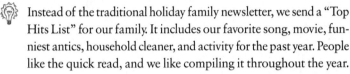 Instead of the traditional holiday family newsletter, we send a "Top Hits List" for our family. It includes our favorite song, movie, funniest antics, household cleaner, and activity for the past year. People like the quick read, and we like compiling it throughout the year.

Inspired by the wonderful book *Night Tree* by Eve Bunting, we go into the mountains and decorate a tree with food for the animals. We use popcorn balls, cranberries, fruit, bread smeared with peanut butter, and birdseed. This is our way of making sure the animals have a special Christmas dinner. Our efforts to change our children's attitudes about what it means to celebrate Christmas have been very successful. December has become such a wonderful time, with gifts nearly an afterthought.

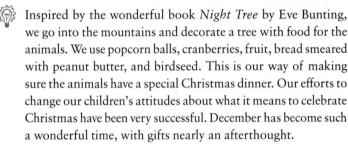

Christmas in 1944 must have been a time of deprivation for many with the war going on and everything being taxed and rationed. But in our small community in northwestern Minnesota, we were no more deprived than usual. We had very little money for gifts and certainly no parties other than family get-togethers—pretty much the usual thing for us.

My grandmother, who had come from Norway in 1900, gave me a surprise gift that year. It was a gold locket, oval in shape with a stylized floral design done with black enamel work. It was, and still is, a beautiful thing. I was twelve years old and thrilled to receive this wonderful gift. She told me it had been in the family for over two hundred years! I had never heard the word heirloom before, but I learned it that year.

Beverly R., Nebraska

We have friends who, having no children to use up their spare cash, generally buy themselves all the things they want throughout the year. Consequently, when Christmas arrives, they already have all the things we might have bought them as presents. A couple of years ago, having racked our brains for what to buy and being on a bit of a budget ourselves, we decided that we would make Christmas baskets for our friends. Each basket contained a homemade cake, homemade biscuits, jam, and pickles, all with personalized labels made on our home computer.

Our friends were so delighted with their homemade gifts, appreciating the time and effort that went into them rather than the cost, that we decided to repeat the "homemade Christmas" the following year with our visiting family members. Everyone who participated had plenty of fun trying to keep the making of the presents a secret, and we amazed each other with our cunning and ingenuity. It took away a lot of the commerciality of Christmas and replaced it with a real family spirit.

Susan N., England

"Let me guess . . . you just got the July issue of Debt-Proof Living!"

14

More Gift Ideas

Face it. If you have a pulse and the ability to sign your name, you don't really have to think much about Christmas gift-giving. Or even read all of these brilliant chapters I've put together for you.

You are free to jump in the car and drive to one of the thousands of mega malls in America where you can swipe the plastic and shop your brains out, buying elaborate gifts for each and every person on your Christmas list. And while you're at it, you might as well have a professional do all your gift wrapping while you put your feet up and sip a lovely coffee drink.

There. Shopping done.

So what's the big deal anyway? And why have I gone to all the effort of suggesting ways you can avoid that kind of Christmas shopping?

May I remind you of a date on the calendar known as January 15? That is about the time when the reality of Christmas sets in as you receive the bills.

If you can barely keep up with your payments now, what makes you think it's going to be any easier to make bigger payments next January? And trust me when I say you are not likely to even remember all the stuff you bought come January 15. And all that expensive wrap? Flapping about in some landfill somewhere.

It's never too late. You still have an option, and that is to get creative. You do not have to spend a lot of money to have the merriest Christmas ever! And you know who's going to be happiest on January 15? You and everyone for whom you spent a little time and created a gift that was unique, useful, and also memorable.

I cannot promise that any of the ideas that follow will hit the bull's-eye for you, but they may stimulate your imagination and help you come up with great ideas of your own.

Gift Ideas for Kids

It's challenging to come up with an original gift for a child that will last longer than the Christmas morning madness.

This year you just might find the solution in a child's custom play kit, a unique assemblage of all the props and accessories necessary for hours of creative and imaginative play. Play kits don't lose their entertainment value, because, unlike some other gifts, they are powered by imagination, not batteries. They spark interest in a child without setting fire to your wallet.

One Debt-Proof Living contributor, Kelly M., wrote how she made a dress-up play kit for her daughter after seeing a really poor quality set for $29.99. That became the first in a series of successful play kits for children. She graciously submitted the following directions and inspiration for ways to make all kinds of play kits.

Play Kits

It takes time and thought to put together a terrific play kit. This is a gift that requires more time than money, so it's never too soon to get started.

First, design the kit on paper by making a list of the contents of your ideal play kit. Go "shopping" in your home, garage, or attic. Let friends, family, and neighbors know what you're looking for too. Ten or twenty dollars will go a long way at your best suppliers: thrift stores, garage sales, consignment stores, and rummage sales.

A note of caution: You cannot be too safe when making play kits for children, especially if you are looking to used goods to make up the kit. If items cannot be sanitized in the laundry, make sure you can have them dry-cleaned or hand washed. Jewelry, accessories, shoes, and so forth should be disinfected using your preferred method of choice. Always err on the side of caution.

Dress-up play kit. You want evening gowns? Women's slips are perfect. Look for fancy lace and lots of color. Short dresses are long gowns on your little one. When it comes to dress-up games, gaudy is better. Sequins, bows, and polka dots are the order of the day. Think bad bridesmaid dresses and New Year's Eve sparkle. Complete the wardrobe with gloves and a hat or two. Maybe even a feather boa or faux fur coat, if you can get one at a good price. Complete the set with cheap costume jewelry and get ready for the fashion shows.

For the little man in your life, start with a man's jacket and a briefcase. Don't forget a few clip-on ties. A pair of overalls and a painter's cap or gardening tools become a handyman's outfit. A fedora and trench coat turns junior into a private detective. Check with your local police department for plastic badges and the airport for flight wings. Add a blue shirt to the badge or wings and you have a pilot or a police officer uniform. Include wallets, watches, a fireman's hat, camouflage pants, and a soldier's cap. Anything that immediately makes you think of a real job is a candidate for the play kit.

Kitchen play kit. Plastic containers are a must. Start with those little pieces that came with your set—you know, the ones you have no earthly use for but can't bear to throw away. This is also a good time to weed out the cups you no longer use and those plastic parfait cups you bought at your neighbor's Tupperware party.

Add gadgets you don't use. You may not need a strawberry huller or a melon baller, but your child will love it. Add wooden spoons, spatulas, and other utensils such as an eggbeater or a cookie press. Most of these items can be found at a thrift store if your kitchen doesn't yield enough goodies. Look for some small pots and skillets. Or choose microwave-safe containers of good, solid plastic that will hold up to rough kitchen play.

Restaurant play kit. Your budding chef may prefer a restaurant to a simple kitchen. Add some dishes, tablecloths, and candleholders to the mix. Keep an eye out for a waitress uniform or a white jacket for the chef. Use your computer to make menus for Cafe Cathy or Johnny's Down Home Diner. Mount them on cardboard and cover them with contact paper so they'll last. You may even want a small blackboard for writing the special of the day.

Don't forget a pad for writing down orders. Actual order pads are inexpensive and available at your local office supply store if you'd like to inject a little more realism into the game. You could even include a bell for "order up" authenticity.

Family play kit. Have a mommy or daddy in training on your hands? You'll need a doll large enough to wear real clothes. You can find baby clothes for as little as a quarter at yard sales, so stock up. Look for sleepers, booties, frilly dresses, and hats. An umbrella-style stroller for $2.95 is superior to a new toy version for $9.99. Add baby bottles, cloth diapers, and a pacifier.

Grocery store play kit. Create a grocery store for running those imaginary errands with baby. This is an easy one since most of the "food" can come straight from your own kitchen.

Start collecting reusable plastic containers such as yogurt cups, butter tubs, and ketchup bottles. Seal the lids with glue. Collect egg cartons, coffee cans, milk jugs, peanut butter jars, and boxes from cereal, pasta, gelatin, pudding, crackers, and other staple items—anything that can be washed and sealed will work great. Firm up cardboard containers by filling them with Styrofoam or rags. Seal them with clear packing tape or contact paper so they'll hold up to frequent use. Rescue and clean plastic fruit for the produce department. Foam rubber is a wonderful material for making slices of bread, vegetables, and other loose foods. Imagination and a few magic markers will fill the store shelves in no time.

Look for inexpensive baskets to combine convenient shopping with storage when the set is not in use. Add a large calculator and play money. Your junior entrepreneur is in business!

Doctor or nurse play kit. Is there a budding doctor or nurse in the house? Create a medical kit. Next time you visit the doctor's office, mention your quest and ask for a donation—a couple of tongue de-pressors, some gauze, or anything to give your set a bit of reality. A white jacket and surgical scrubs can be found in a used uniform store if your thrift shop doesn't have them. Find a clipboard and file folders to make medical charts.

A sphygmomanometer, otherwise known as a blood pressure cuff, can be made with a piece of black felt, Velcro, and plastic tubing. The bulb end can be made from the end of a turkey baster or the bulb from a bike horn.

Handyman play kit. Fill a tool chest with screwdrivers, a hammer, and a socket set (who cares if it's missing a piece or two?). Throw in a broken clock to take apart and put back together. Pieces of wood, screws, nuts, and bolts will spark an older child's curiosity and creativity. Think child safety before including small items or things with cords or of an electrical nature. Use a cooler or suitcase as the tool chest to keep prices down and pieces together. And if you're worried about too many little pieces, it's no worse than stepping on a Lego block.

Homekeeping play kit. Keeping house is a chore to adults but looks like fun to most kids. Develop their interest early by giving them their own cleaning tools. Look for a carpet sweeper or handheld vacuum. A travel iron (remove the cord) and tabletop ironing board are child-sized versions of the real thing. Add a bucket and sponges, a few rags, and a feather duster. How about a child-sized rake, garden tools, and play lawn mower to add to the fun? Label empty plastic spray bottles with "window cleaner" and "furniture polish." Remember to seal the bottles if you want them to stay empty.

Entertainment play kit. Hollywood awaits your budding filmmaker. All you need is a nonworking (or working if you can get a deal) video camera and some crazy props. A girl dressed in evening clothes would love to be the star of the latest production.

Make a clapboard of cardboard or foam board. Raid Halloween costumes to create the wardrobe department. A microphone can be used for live news reports one day and sold-out concerts the next. The camera goes on location for a wild (stuffed) animal safari today and shoots music videos tomorrow.

Unleash your imagination. If you can imagine it, so can your child. Cowboys, construction workers, and auto mechanics can fill out costume sets. A stuffed animal collection surely needs a zookeeper or veterinarian. A chalkboard and some textbooks mean school is in session any time. A set can be as large or small as space and materials will allow.

If you believe storage will be a problem with some of these play kits, make sure storage is a part of the gift itself. A suitcase or old trunk is the perfect accompaniment to any dress-up kit. Housekeeping tools can be packed into a laundry basket. Use a large plastic container for the store or kitchen sets. Store baby's supplies in a large diaper bag. A fishing tackle box makes a great toolbox. You get the idea.

More Gifts for Kids

Books as well as books on CD are always welcome gifts for kids of all ages. Ask your librarian or an elementary school teacher for recommendations.

Personalize a book-of-the-month gift by either writing and designing the book yourself or buying an inexpensive one that reflects the appropriate holiday or season.

For a young girl who loves to play dress-up, cover a shoe box with pretty wrapping paper inside and out. Fill it with inexpensive makeup and costume jewelry. Hint: All of the makeup at EyesLipsFace.com costs a dollar per item and comes packaged in smaller containers—perfect for the younger set.

A homemade balance beam with proper supports is perfect for an aspiring gymnast. Make sure you start with sturdy material, then sand and finish the surfaces.

An appliance box, with doors and windows cut out and decorated to look like a house, castle, office, or school, is always a big hit. This idea is in accordance with the rule that says the bigger and more expensive the toy, the more likely the child will want to play with the box it came in.

Fill a piggy bank with starter money.

Make your own play dough. Combine in a saucepan 1 cup flour, ½ cup salt, 1 cup water, 1 tablespoon vegetable oil, 2 teaspoons cream of tartar, and food coloring. Mix and cook over medium heat, stirring constantly, until a ball is formed. Pour onto a floured board or wax paper and knead until smooth. Tightly covered, it will keep for several weeks.

Create a simplified map of the town in which the child lives. Highlight the location of significant landmarks: the child's school, church, Daddy's and Mommy's offices, the zoo, and the library.

Kids love to create little books with coupons in them, good for things such as one night's dishwashing or a kiss and a hug. Parents can give reverse coupons to their kids—good for exemptions from making their beds, setting the table, and so on.

Give tickets to a favorite sporting event or for a ride on a real train (accompanied by an adult, of course).

Yarn, needles, a beginner's book, and a certificate for knitting lessons from the giver are very popular these days.

A simple camera, a photo album, and lessons on how to download pictures to the family's computer printer will spark creativity.

Make a one-of-a-kind puzzle. Mount an enlarged photo of yourself or some family occasion onto a piece of foam board (available at stationery or art supply stores). Cover the photo with a piece of tracing paper and lightly draw a jigsaw pattern, making as many or as few pieces as would be appropriate for the age of the recipient. Using a sharp knife (such as an X-ACTO), carefully cut through the tissue paper, photo, and board along the puzzle lines. Separate the pieces and place in a gift box.

Preschoolers love puzzles. Lay a strip of masking tape on a table, sticky side up. Press about ten popsicle sticks (or wooden tongue depressors) side by side evenly across the tape. Draw a picture and write the child's name on the sticks. Then remove the tape and shuffle the sticks to make a great puzzle.

For an artist's box, start with a clear storage box (a twelve-quart box is a good size). Write the child's name on it and fill it with plain white paper, construction paper, crayons, colored pencils, glue, tape, a ruler, plastic stencils, and a pencil sharpener.

Start a collection of Christmas tree ornaments for a child, to be added to each year.

A beginner stamp-collector kit from the US Postal Service is great for children. These kits are quite inexpensive, impressive, and are geared toward the young philatelist.

Gift Ideas for Teenagers

Give a night on the town with an envelope of cash labeled for fast food, a movie, and the ice-cream shop—or Starbucks. Or get gift cards for each (following the cautions provided in chapter 8). This is a gift a teen will love.

Make an appointment for a beauty makeover at a local school of cosmetology. Prices are typically very inexpensive, and all the work done by students is closely supervised. Stick with temporary work such as hairstyling, manicures, pedicures, and facials and stay away from haircuts and color.

Here's a list of other ideas for teens:

Calligraphy pen and instruction book.

Knitting supplies, pattern, and instructional DVD.

With parental permission, a makeup case for the soon-to-be teen filled with lip gloss, nail polish, bubble bath, dusting powder, and a light scent.

Self-help and inspirational books.

Devotionals.

Calendar.

Picture frame or empty photo album.

Body pillow or decorative pillows for the bed.

Desk accessories.

Hobby equipment.

Framed print or poster for a teen's bedroom wall.

Cell phone case.

Movie tickets.

An additional piece of whatever the teen collects.

Currency taped in a pleasing arrangement and then slipped into a picture frame that has glass on which you have written "just in case of emergency."

Journal or diary.

Money.

Board game.

3-D puzzles.

Gift Ideas for College Students

Send a Christmas basket to a college student on the first of December. Include a holiday CD and decorations for the dorm room. Christmas cards, stamps, and red and green pens are just a few more ideas.

Food. Anything that can be kept in a dorm, sorority, or frat room. A small appliance that is not restricted in a group living situation.

Make or purchase an oversized laundry bag with the recipient's name on the front. Fill with detergent, fabric softener, bleach, and a roll of quarters. Add a couple of magazines for the laundromat wait.

Gift Ideas for Adults

Foolproof recipes are always welcome gifts. Copy twenty of your favorite recipes into a notebook. Add a personal note as appropriate.

Set aside two hours a week to serve as chauffeur, escort, or errand runner for a special person who doesn't drive or doesn't have time to get to the library, grocery store, pharmacy, dry cleaner, post office, etc.

Offer to keep children of young parents overnight once a month or once a quarter. Arrange to pick them up in the mid-afternoon so the parents can enjoy the evening together.

Offer to care for a pet during a vacation.

Give a dinner a month to an overworked mom. Offer a piping-hot and ready-to-eat casserole once a month. She can specify her busiest evening.

Make a beautiful watering can for a plant or garden lover on your gift list. Either buy a new watering can or give an old one a face-lift. You'll need some self-adhesive shelf liner or covering and a pair of scissors. Cut the covering into a strip to wrap around the handle, another for the water spout, then larger pieces for the can itself. Peel away the backing and carefully wrap the entire can. The end result: a functional watering can that's pretty enough to be used as a vase.

Make a collage or memory box for a person who made a special trip with you. Arrange postcards, ticket stubs, foreign currency, luggage tags, airline boarding passes, and street maps and combine with photos of the trip.

Fill a blue basket with a variety of blueberry products such as jam, muffin and pancake mix, and syrup; blueberry-scented candles, bath salts, and room freshener; and blue notepaper. The same idea can be used for strawberry, lavender, peppermint, or other flavors.

To turn a plain cookie sheet into a fancy bistro tray, glue on canceled foreign stamps and/or domestic commemorative stamps. Cover the entire tray, then apply several coats of polyurethane varnish.

Everyone has a box or two of old family photographs. For a special vintage touch, choose a black-and-white photo that has special meaning for the recipient. You can frame it in its original form or have a photocopy enlargement made at a copy store. An inexpensive black or silver frame will turn this treasure into an heirloom.

Make a working woman's emergency kit: a small Swiss Army knife; a good lint roller (a pet-hair remover from a pet store is the best bargain); an assortment of safety pins, needles, and thread; Kiwi's Shine Wipes (instant shoeshines); double-stick tape to fix hems in a hurry; small scissors; a glue stick (better than clear nail polish for arresting a hosiery run); antistatic spray; several pencil erasers (the tiny eraser from a pencil makes a dandy temporary replacement for the back of a pierced earring). Put everything in a small, compact container, such as a pretty box or fabric bag.

Offer an evening of babysitting to someone who cannot afford a babysitter.

Go to a magazine stand and select a magazine you know someone would enjoy, maybe because of a hobby or a secret desire—to sail or skydive, for example. Wrap the magazine with a note saying "Look forward to this all next year!" Be sure to mail in the subscription card with a check.

Give a wicker bed tray or other container filled with fixings for breakfast in bed—muffin mix, jams or jellies, coffee beans, plus a subscription to a favorite newspaper.

Books make great gifts. But don't limit yourself to shopping in the big chains. Secondhand bookstores are less expensive and often have out-of-print titles that can't be found elsewhere. Also, these stores may sell old prints or maps that would reflect personal interests and be suitable for framing.

Pass along an heirloom to the next generation. Write up the history of the heirloom and encourage the recipient to display, use, and enjoy this new treasure.

Make an appointment for a beauty makeover for a young mother (massage, facial, and manicure) at a local beauty college. Volunteer to take care of the kids.

Gather old family movies, take them to a camera shop, and have them transferred to DVD.

Share a cord of firewood with a neighbor. Announce the gift in a card tucked between several logs wrapped with a wide ribbon. If possible, stack the wood between your properties.

A video makes a very special holiday greeting or gift. Put together a movie with highlights of the past year. Include birthday celebrations, summer vacation footage, sporting events, a school play, and other special moments. A festive way to end the movie is to gather the family and sing "We Wish You a Merry Christmas." A video or DVD like this will bring joy to faraway family members long after Christmas has come and gone.

Gift Ideas for Senior Citizens

An adult child can give date-a-month coupons to a parent. A man setting aside time to spend alone with his mother, or an adult daughter taking her dad out once a month, is a lovely gesture. Some months your evening together could include a movie, other times, just dinner and time to talk and listen.

Take Grandma or Grandpa on a movie date. Pick them up and treat them to a night out. If they prefer, rent a movie and bring snacks.

Give a book on CD to a senior citizen whose eyes are failing. Wrap with a small headset and CD player. Lend him or her your CDs and offer to include a trip to the library for more.

For an elderly person with failing vision, give a subscription to the *New York Times Large Print Weekly*, which offers a select package of the week's news printed in 16-point type—about twice the size of the regular type. The cost as of this writing was $1.65 or $3.30 per week, depending on delivery method. For more information, call 800-698-4637 or go to http://homedelivery.nytimes.com, scroll to the bottom of the page, and look for "You may also like." In that box, select "Large Print Weekly."

Fill a pretty box with a variety of greeting cards, a pen, and a roll of postage stamps for someone who is housebound.

Give a photo album to grandparents filled with pictures of baby's typical day—morning bath, breakfast, taking a walk, playing, greeting Daddy, being rocked to sleep. Update photos throughout the year as baby grows and the days are more eventful. A video recording in which baby is the star is also a terrific gift.

Gifts for Specific Enthusiasts

For baseball and sports enthusiasts. The Hall of Fame museum store, Cooperstown, New York, offers baseball collectibles, memberships, certificates, uniforms, T-shirts, and unique baseball items; Baseball halloffame.org; 888-425-5633. Fogdog Sports represents and carries all major brands and major sports categories. Items range from socks to official jerseys; Fogdog.com; 800-624-2017.

For nature enthusiasts. Check out the National Park Service and National Park Bookshop for everything from annual park passes to books and gift items; NPS.gov.

For game enthusiasts. This company sells every game that's new and in print. It doesn't sell out-of-print games but features links to sites that will find and sell out-of-print and used games; GamePreserve .com; 800-414-2637.

For space enthusiasts. The Kennedy Space Center online store features gifts, trinkets, toys, educational materials, and memorabilia; KennedySpaceCenter.com; 321-449-4444.

Everything you can think of with a space theme, such as talking lunar landers, NASA items, astronaut memorabilia, CDs, and games, can be found at Thespacestore.com; 877-698-0704.

For cowboy enthusiasts. The world's largest western store offers western wear, hats, chaps, boots, even spurs; Sheplers.com; 888-835-4004.

For museum enthusiasts. The San Francisco Exploratorium's online store is full of fascinating things in every price range to look at, play with, and learn from for everyone from toddlers to teenagers to so-called grown-ups; Exploratoriumstore.com; 415-397-5673. Also, the Smithsonian Institute has a wonderful catalog as well as online store; www.SmithsonianStore.com; 866-945-6897.

For philatelic enthusiasts. Subway Stamp is the world's largest stamp and coin-collecting supply and information company; Subwaystamp .com; 800-221-9960. The United States Postal Service offers stamps, supplies, stamp-collecting kits, gifts, and more in most of its post offices as well as online at USPS.com; click on "Store."

For doll enthusiasts. The American Girl Store features books, doll clothing and accessories, event information and tickets, tours, and dolls; AmericanGirlStore.com; 800-360-1861. You will find dolls and accessories for every occasion and at every price range at edolls.com; 973-275-0041.

For airplane enthusiasts. Find high-quality transportation collectibles and the most extensive selection of aviation videos, books, and kits; Airplaneshop.com; 800-752-6346. Find all types of high-performance paper airplanes and gliders; Whitewings.com; 800-233-7174.

For philanthropy enthusiasts. Choose a gift that changes lives: essential needs, good health, nourishing food, training, education, empowering families, and handcrafted items; Worldvisiongifts.org; 888-511-6548.

Kits are available for you or your organization to assemble: school kits, health kits, clean-up kits, and baby kits; Churchworldservice .org; 888-297-2767.

For weather enthusiasts. Twister Enterprises loves tornadoes and twisters. They have captured this phenomenon of nature in one of their products, the Pet Tornado; Explore4fun.com; 303-499-1716.

For tea enthusiasts. Adagio Teas is a unique company that carries teas from all over the world. Find gift sets, international teas, herbal teas, tea accessories, expert recommendations, and more; Adagio.com.

For cooking enthusiasts. This site's gift center features favorite equipment at every price range and discounts on many items for birthdays, kids, and gourmet gift baskets. Items are also categorized by interests and hobbies, occasions and events, and departments. They'll even gift wrap; Cooking.com; 800-663-8810.

Online shopping safety reminder: Always consider that shipping and handling costs are part of the purchase price. Know what they are before you make your final decision. Pay only with a personal credit card, never a debit card, business credit card, or check. Only a personal credit card provides the consumer protection you need when ordering online.

When you make a purchase, enter the full amount into your checkbook as if you'd written a check for that amount, and deduct it from the balance.

After completing the transaction and before leaving the website, print out the details about your order and specific information about the merchant just in case the page disappears or you forget how you found it in the first place.

More Gift Ideas

Here are more gift ideas contributed by faithful fans and clever members of Debt-Proof Living online.

 One year I got the best gift. My mother is an excellent cook and often cooks without a recipe. My sister spent hours with her in the kitchen and painstakingly recorded the exact ingredients and measurements for our favorite dishes. She transferred them to a permanent recipe book for me. I cherish this gift not only because my sister made it for me but also because these recipes are now recorded for us to pass on and will always remind us of our mother.

 My sister kept a T-shirt from every school event she ever participated in. For a gift, I cut out the pattern/words from each shirt and made her a memory quilt. I used her favorite color for the border and inexpensive materials for the backing. It wasn't too expensive, but it was time-consuming. She loves it.

During the year, I collect old salt and pepper shakers (from yard sales, estate sales, tag sales, junk stores). Tied with a pretty bow and filled with perfumed body powder, they make useful little gifts. I make the powder by adding a few drops of my favorite perfume to cornstarch. I leave the mixture in a covered bowl for several days so the cornstarch absorbs the wonderful fragrance.

 Seashell gifts are increasingly popular for those who live by the sea and those who wish they did. Buy a bag of shells from your local craft or dollar store. Go to the hardware store and buy some button-style night-lights (General Electric makes a long-lasting model for about two dollars). Superglue a larger shell to the night-light to make an attractive, unique night-light. Fan-shaped shells have been the favorite of my gift recipients.

 I love to give gift cards that I know my recipients will appreciate, but I always add a little something extra—usually homemade. For example, for a gift card to a bookstore I'll include a book-mark I've sewn or cross-stitched. A gift card to a craft store would be wrapped in a small storage container or tied to a craft I've made. With a certificate for Chinese food I might wrap up fortune cookies I've made myself (a quick internet search will turn up a recipe or two) into which I've inserted personalized and humorous fortunes. With a gift card to a nursery I would include a pot of forced paperwhites. A gift card is best when it comes with something memorable.

 Think consumables. Consumables are gifts that will be used up, not stashed in a closet for the next yard sale. Here's an example: Forget the Easy-Bake Oven, a pricey toy that promises to bake cookies using a single light bulb. Instead, bundle a few cookie cutters, a mini rolling pin, and a box of sugar cookie mix together with a certificate for cookie lessons. Magazine subscriptions, food, theater tickets, and personal care items are all examples of consumables—items that are enjoyed while being used up.

 Last Christmas my husband and I were new parents and very short on cash. Both sets of grandparents and all the uncles and aunts were thrilled with the inexpensive gifts we created. We purchased ceramic tiles from a hobby store (also sold at home-improvement stores) and bought a couple of tubes of the bake-on paint that becomes permanent after you bake it in your oven. Our daughter contributed her handprints to the personalized tiles. I don't think a store-bought gift would have been even half as special.

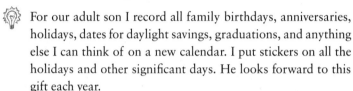 For our adult son I record all family birthdays, anniversaries, holidays, dates for daylight savings, graduations, and anything else I can think of on a new calendar. I put stickers on all the holidays and other significant days. He looks forward to this gift each year.

Attending a wedding during the summer or fall season? Need a present for the bridal shower or wedding day? Consider a unique gift of holiday Christmas ornaments. Keep in mind the decorating taste and style of the couple, and if you're not sure stick with simplicity: white lights, silver and gold Christmas balls, and an "our first Christmas together" ornament with wedding date and names of the bride and groom. It will give that first Christmas a nice start.

A wonderful and inexpensive idea for a Christmas gift to a parent is to write, typeset, and frame a tribute to them.

Shop throughout the year for glass containers on clearance racks, at garage sales, and even at dollar stores. Make your own lotion for gifts and prepare about one week ahead to allow time for settling. Add a cute ribbon for an original, inexpensive, and useful gift. Lotion ingredients: 16 ounces Unibase (order from pharmacy), 16 ounces glycerin (also at the pharmacy), and 5 cups distilled water. Place ingredients in a large bowl and mix well by hand. In another bowl, beat 2 cups at a time for ten seconds. Keep in a cool place until it settles. Transfer to gift bottles.

Last summer I bought a wildflower carpet for half price in the garden department. I wasn't sure how successful it would be, but to my surprise it bloomed like crazy this spring. I am now harvesting the seeds, and for Christmas I'll be giving wildflower seed mix. I have at least seven varieties of seeds to put in the mix and will package them in pretty bottles or decorative envelopes with planting directions included. I have enough seeds for ten or more gifts and plenty for my garden next year too.

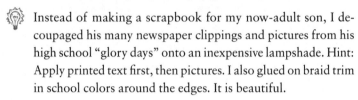 Instead of making a scrapbook for my now-adult son, I decoupaged his many newspaper clippings and pictures from his high school "glory days" onto an inexpensive lampshade. Hint: Apply printed text first, then pictures. I also glued on braid trim in school colors around the edges. It is beautiful.

My mother and I received the best gift from my sister last year. Using a vintage black-and-white photo from the '50s, she had two iron-on transfer photos made at Kinko's. She ironed each onto muslin, then applied the transfer to patchwork pillow covers she made. The pillows were designed to complement our home décor. These pillows were especially meaningful because the photo was of my sis and me holding hands with Santa (secretly performed by our late father).

My daughter is a commercial airline pilot and has few needs or wants. Last Christmas we gave her a memory jar. I had all her siblings, nephews, and friends give me their special memories of her. As these came in, I entered them on my computer. Every time my husband or I would remember something I would do the same. I started with my first memory of her at birth and went from there. Some were hilarious, others quite serious. By Christmas we had over eighty-six memories. I printed them out on colored paper, folded them accordion-style, and put them in a glass jar with a poem I wrote attached to the outside. She tells me that on days when she is feeling blue she goes to the jar and pulls out a memory. It always perks her up.

Last year I gave my daughter and her husband a large jar filled with quarters I saved over the year. As apartment dwellers on a tight budget, they were really happy to see enough quarters in that jar to do their laundry for a year!

I purchase plain coffee mugs and personalize them for Christmas gifts using a pen designed for writing on ceramic. I write or draw appropriate messages and, following the instructions on the pen, bake the mugs in the oven. For a friend who now lives far away I wrote, "Even though we are far apart, we can still have coffee together!"

 My elderly neighbor who's on a fixed income recently shared with me her great idea for Christmas gifts for her thirty grandkids. She is buying each child a five-dollar gift card from Dollar Tree along with a promise that Gran will take them there alone with her to shop and spend their gift. That should take up the entire month of January easily. She will get to spend some time with each of the grandkids, and they can get whatever appeals to them.

 Last Christmas I took a vintage black-and-white photo of my great-grandmother to my local copy store and had copies made of it. I printed her favorite poem on marbled paper stock and bought matching three-dollar frames (one for each of my family members). I positioned a photo and poem in each frame and for just six dollars each gave something all of us will treasure forever.

 I have sewn and crafted for years and find the best gifts are ones that are personalized. At Christmas nothing beats a miniature stocking or small fabric drawstring bag with the name of the recipient on the cuff and a small gift tucked inside such as bubble bath, a scented candle, or something that is of particular interest for the recipient.

 Family memories to me are priceless, so this is the gift I will be giving this year. I will sit down with our family photo albums and narrate the stories behind the pictures. My children are always asking me what life was like when I was a child or before I met Daddy. My gift will be a guided tour of my life and theirs as babies. I am going to make a CD to go with each album. Another gift idea would be to photocopy the albums and duplicate the CD so each family member has his or her own copy.

This year I'm having my dad's police officer patch turned into a blanket (scanned and printed out on the blanket). This can be done for business logos, college insignias, professional organizations, sports teams, etc. This does take a little time to research, so it's good to start early.

Some people say giving money as a gift is tacky, but it is not. Money always fits. It's never the wrong color, and it works in any store or bank account. Unlike a gift card, the recipient can spend cash right to the very last penny. Sales of Hallmark greeting cards that are designed to hold cash have increased so dramatically in the past few years that they are now a top seller, evidence that currency is still in vogue and quite acceptable.

Select a cookbook and choose a recipe from the book. Attach a card to the front that includes the recipe name and page number. Place the cookbook and dry ingredients for the recipe in a decorative basket.

Use your computer. Make a set of thank-you notes or stationery; tie with a festive ribbon and place in an attractive tin for that one-of-a-kind gift. Don't forget to include a colorful pen and envelopes.

Holiday flowers. Find amaryllis, paperwhites, poinsettias, and English ivy during the holidays at a nursery or home-improvement center. Placed in an attractive, decorative container, they make a great holiday gift.

One Christmas I was at a loss for what to give my friends and family. I was short on cash and would not use my credit card. I was at a Hallmark store with a friend. There on the counter were some pretty rocks with words carved into them. I started thinking it would be nice to personalize something like that for friends and family—so I did!

I went to a craft store and bought some little paper boxes for 99 cents each. I then bought a bag of river rock for $5.00. I made a list of ten things that I treasured about each family member and friend and then decorated a box for each with their favorite things on the outside using stickers and stamps I had at home. I wrote each person's name and "Treasure Box" on the outside. I washed the rocks and then used a felt-tip marker to write on the stones the things I treasured about that person. Then I decoupaged each stone.

I packaged the stones in the decorated boxes with colored tissue paper and some candy. I made up a tag that said, "Inside you will find ten things I treasure about you. I hope you will use this treasure box when you are feeling down to realize how much I care about you. I also hope you will add your own treasures to the box and remember to live with joy!"

Everyone flipped for this gift! Most said it was the best gift they had ever received. This was a gift for me too, as I was able to take time to think about the wonderful people in my life and how much I cherish them as I wrote their "treasures" on the stones. This was a project that was inexpensive, easy, and gave so much back.

Elaine O., California

15

Wrap It Up!

A great place to cut back on the cost of Christmas is gift wrap. In fact, depending on the supplies you have available already, there's a very good chance you can get through the season without purchasing any gift-wrapping materials at all. Just look around the house and you'll be amazed at what you can turn into creative gift wrap filled with personality and attitude.

Trust me, three days before Christmas is not the time to start thinking about ways to wrap gifts and decorate the house creatively (read: cheaply). In fact, that's the dangerous time when the crush of the season erases all thoughts of frugality—when the just-gotta-get-it-done pressure sets in and all sense of reason disappears.

Following are great tips and tricks I've collected over the years.

Gift Wrapping

Set up a gift-wrapping area. Drape a card table or other surface with a large tablecloth or sheet that hangs to the floor. This is important so you can hide wrapping supplies under the table for quick retrieval.

Sew little pouches of red or green velvet, put small gifts inside, and tie with a holiday ribbon.

Outsmart kids who are prone to snooping by wrapping gifts before you hide them. Instead of using tags, put a color-coded, self-stick dot on each package so only you know who gets the gift.

Turn ordinary shoe boxes into colorful gift boxes. Use an X-ACTO knife to cut simple designs such as stars on the sides and top of the box. Paint the box with brightly colored acrylic paint. Wrap the gift in tissue paper of a contrasting color and let it show through the cutouts.

Brown (kraft) paper is not just for mailing packages. Dressed up with stickers, doilies, fancy ribbon, and such, it's a wonderfully inexpensive way to wrap gifts. You can either purchase kraft paper in a roll or recycle brown grocery bags. To remove creases from folded or wrinkled kraft and other types of wrapping paper, lightly press them out with your iron, set on the lowest setting. Don't steam the paper. For persistent wrinkles, spray the wrong side lightly with spray starch. Don't attempt to iron waxed or foil paper.

Instead of buying expensive holiday wrapping paper, purchase a large roll of white butcher paper and a bolt of red plaid ribbon from a florist supply store.

Start saving the comics from the Sunday paper now and by Christmas you will have a good supply. You can also use foreign newspapers, the sports section, or fashion ads. All make clever gift wrap.

Make a Santa sack for each of your children or, if you are ambitious, each member of the family. Sew together two large panels of Christmas fabric (approximately one yard each) on three sides, add a drawstring to the top, drop in the gifts from Santa, attach a name tag, and place the sack under the tree. You can explain that the elves are much too tired to wrap after making all those toys. These Santa sacks can be reused every year, which will create a new family tradition.

If you use a plain-colored box, wrap only the lid. It saves paper and makes the gift easier to open. If the box is not plain, wrap the box and lid separately. It's easier to open and allows the box to be reused.

Find paper that's appropriate for the gift or recipient. For example, wrap a cookbook with pages from a beautiful food magazine or use sheet music for a music lover's package.

Save your kids' drawings and use them to wrap gifts. Tape several together if the package is large. This will be a big hit, especially with grandparents.

Snip sponges into fun shapes, then dab in poster paint and press in a decorative pattern on the insides of brown paper grocery bags that have been cut open. This also works well for decorating cards and invitations.

Wrap odd-shaped packages in new handkerchiefs that become part of the gift.

Cut two matching tree shapes out of felt to cover a tall bottle holding herbed vinegar or maple syrup. Sew or glue the sides together, leaving the bottom open. Then cut out felt ornaments and glue them onto the tree.

Place a gift box diagonally on a square scarf and tie opposite corners together at the top. Tie again with gold cord or ribbon.

Wrap a box in brown paper, then hot glue rows of pennies to the outside in a symmetrical design, randomly, or in the shape of a Christmas tree. Tie with a copper-colored or white ribbon.

If a gift is really large, don't waste yards and yards of pricey paper. Put those cans of spray paint sitting in the garage to use and paint the carton, then add a bow.

A car, or even a bicycle, can be "wrapped" by tying an oversized gift tag to a piece of string. Leave the tag under the tree and run the string to where the gift awaits—in a closet, the basement, the attic, or even the garage.

If a gift is just too cumbersome to wrap at all, didn't arrive in time for Christmas, or didn't quite get finished, wrap a smaller box containing a clue about the gift to come, plus a claim check for redeeming it.

If the paper doesn't quite fit the package, try laying the item diagonally on the paper so the corners can be folded toward the center.

If time is short or gift wrapping is especially difficult, use a white plastic trash bag (two if they are too transparent) tied with a great big bow. With presents, as with people, it's what's inside that counts. And now you have armed your recipient with the perfect receptacle for cleanup too.

You can purchase pastel and brightly colored paper lunch bags very cheaply at a discount store. Decorate and use them for gift bags.

Wrap a gift in tissue and place it in the bag. Fold the top of the bag down and punch two holes through all thicknesses. Thread a ribbon through the holes, then tie a bow or add curling ribbon.

Coffee cans with plastic lids (both small and large sizes) make terrific gift containers. Simply tape or glue a piece of colorful paper to the outside of the can. Top with a bow or raffia.

Many magazine ad pages make terrific wrapping paper for DVDs and other small objects. Try to match the selection with the personality of the person receiving the gift. Great magazines to consider are *Martha Stewart Living*, Oprah's *O*, and *Real Simple*. Top with a treatment of cord or narrow ribbon.

You can wrap a box with a new scarf, towel, tablecloth, or other piece of fabric. Now the wrapping becomes part of the gift itself.

Old road maps make perfect gift wrap for a traveler or remind the recipient of a favorite trip.

Print your own wrapping paper. Visit the "Activity Center" at websites such as HP.com to find free printouts of gift-wrap designs and gift boxes that you can fold yourself using the instructions the site provides. Once at the site, click on "Explore & Create," next "At Home," then "Project Types." You'll discover lots of fun, exciting, and free projects.

Spray paint a bag. Cut open several large paper grocery bags or some kraft paper and crumple it several times. Then flatten it out and use spray paint to color the paper. (It is best to spray the paint at an angle.) Let the paper dry before you store it. You won't even have to worry about it getting wrinkled.

Use your paper shredder to make your own basket filling. Once you have placed your gifts inside, you can shrink-wrap the basket yourself. Just purchase some inexpensive shrink-wrap from a craft store and use your blow-dryer to heat the wrap.

Tags, Trims, and Cards

Visit a decorator fabric shop, upholstery supply store, or sewing supply store and look for braids, cordings, tiebacks, fringes, and tassels to use instead of ribbon. Bolt ends are often sold as remnants at just a fraction of their retail price.

Tie a couple of pieces of a child's favorite candy (wrapped in colored plastic wrap) to the outside of a gift.

Use new, colored, or patterned shoelaces to tie up small packages. Add jingle bells for that special touch.

Recycle old Christmas cards to make gift tags. Cut out a part of the design, punch a hole, and tie it on.

Any all-cotton fabric will tear into lengths of "ribbon." Allow the edges to fray and you will have an amazingly beautiful presentation. Use homespun fabric (this means the pattern is woven in, not printed on one side) "ribbon" on plain brown paper wrap for a beautiful country look.

Cut strips of wrapping paper and curl them with the edge of a scissors blade the same way you would curling ribbon. This requires a gentle touch so the paper ribbon does not tear, but the final effect is lovely.

Stop by a local print shop and ask for any scraps of colored paper they are discarding. Use green paper to make holly leaves. Add tiny red berries cut from red scraps, and you have beautiful gift tags. Make blue stars and yellow bells. The possibilities are endless.

Using holiday-shaped cookie cutters as a pattern, cut tags from file folders or other heavy card stock. Decorate with stickers, markers, or rubber stamps.

Recycle silver-lined mylar potato chip and popcorn bags into gift ribbon. Wash them carefully to remove all traces of salt and oil. With scissors, cut one long ribbon of your desired width, starting at the top and spiraling around the bag. Curl as you would regular curling ribbon.

Instead of writing a recipient's name on the tag, attach a childhood photo. It's fun for kids to try to match the grown-ups with the pictures.

Get a marking pen that writes on glossy surfaces (Sharpie is a popular brand; check stationery and art supply stores), and you can skip the gift tags entirely.

Just in case the tags fall off packages under the tree or while in transit, write the names of the recipients on the back of the wrapped gifts.

Don't throw away those wrinkled gift bows. You can reuse them by placing the bows in the dryer along with a damp washcloth. Set the machine on "fluff" or "air dry" for two minutes. The bows will come out looking like new.

Make your own stamps with Christmas symbols for hand-decorated cards and gift tags. Draw a pattern on the wide end of a cork. With an X-ACTO knife or similar sharp instrument, carefully cut the cork away from the design to a depth of about a quarter of an inch. Stamp the cork onto an ink pad and press down hard on the paper. Because corks are small, so are the images; therefore, plan to make lots of different simple shapes such as hearts, stars, and trees.

Send postcards instead of traditional Christmas cards. They are cheaper to mail, and a clever sender can create one by recycling last year's cards.

If you have a very long Christmas card list and feel rushed to write the personal notes you love so much, divide your list over four or five holidays such as Valentine's Day, Easter, Halloween, Thanksgiving, and Christmas. Explain that this is your annual greeting. To keep your records straight, color code every name in your address book to indicate on which holiday you wrote the note.

For the natural look, pinecones, sea shells, dried flowers, and seed pods can all become decorations for the top of a package. Glue pressed flowers onto small squares of paper for a pretty gift tag to finish it off.

Dress up a gift with a tag that can double as a necklace. Get a mini brass hinge at the hardware store—the type of hinge that has two equally shaped sides that fold in the middle. See how it looks like a tiny book? Glue two pieces of colored paper to fit the front and back of the hinge. Glue a strip of paper to fit inside the "book." Decorate the cover with tiny beads, stickers, or a drawing. Allow to dry, then write a message inside. Fold ribbon in half to make a loop. Thread the ribbon ends through one of the screw holes, then through the ribbon loop. Pull snug. Knot ends. Attach it to the gift with a note that says it would make a dandy necklace.

Decorate gifts with ribbon alternatives. Plastic pearl necklaces (Mardi Gras beads) make festive ribbon. You can also curl long, thin strips of colored paper just like ribbon and tape them to the top of a package.

Make sealing wax tags. Tear off a small square of foil and place it on the table. Melt some wax and let it drop in a puddle on the foil. Quickly take a decorative button or stamp and press it into the wax.

Peel the button or stamp off and let the wax dry. Add some hot glue to the back and attach it to a ribbon. Then attach the ribbon to the gift.

Prepare for Shipping

When you need to pad a package, recycle whatever you can. Instead of bubble wrap and Styrofoam, use newspaper. If you or someone you know has a paper shredder, save a bagful of the shreddings. Use stale, air-popped—not buttered—popcorn and include a note instructing the recipients to keep the gift and give the popcorn to the birds.

Cut empty wrapping paper tubes to fit inside a box you are mailing. They cushion the contents but add little weight.

Cut a brown paper bag to accommodate the item you're sending. Using heavy tape, seal three of the sides. Slip the gift into the mailer, provide padding as necessary, and tape up the fourth side.

Don't use shoe boxes for mailing, because they tend to split.

If you use Styrofoam peanuts as a packing cushion, spritz them with an antistatic spray first.

The US Postal Service says address labels should be legible from thirty inches away. That's about an arm's length.

Mark packages that contain breakables as "fragile" in three places: above the address, below the postage, and on the reverse side.

Use filament-reinforced tape to seal packages for shipping. Do not use twine, string, or cord—they will get caught in automation equipment.

As you unwrap gifts this year, save discarded paper, ribbon, and packing materials to use as packing material for next year.

Enclose a piece of paper inside the box with the address of the recipient and yours as the return.

Just before you seal up a box for mailing, sprinkle in some pine-scented potpourri. When your recipient opens the carton, the whole room will smell like Christmas.

If you write an address directly on a box, use a waterproof marker.

Mail early. Avoid the temptation or requirement to upgrade to a faster shipping method. It really hurts when the postage exceeds the cost of what's inside.

Consider the environment and your wallet before throwing mountains of used wrapping materials into the trash. There are so many ways to give paper a new life rather than sending it to the landfill. Some types of paper can be shredded to use for animal bedding or for packaging material you'll need in the coming year. Or reuse paper for the purpose it was created in the first place: as gift wrap! Taking a little time to deal with it now could save you a lot of time and money in the future.

One year around April, I started squeezing out thirty dollars per month from our monthly budget. I would set the cash aside in an envelope, hidden from everyone. I had to have the actual cash on hand, because it is more tempting for me to spend money if I can simply transfer it from a savings account to my checking account.

In late November, I started collecting lists from everyone and watching ads. When an opportunity presented itself, I purchased the gift with the cash. We were able to add a little extra to the fund in December (about one hundred dollars), and the bottom line was everyone had a great Christmas. We were able to purchase many items on everyone's lists, and we didn't have any debt to pay off. We did have a small budget, but no one felt slighted. There were still surprises, and we had enough for the neighbors and teachers at our church. My thirteen-year-old son said it was the best Christmas ever.

L.N., email

Because my husband and I both have large families, we decided that for each other we would only exchange ornaments for our tree. The ornaments could be store-bought or homemade. The key was to give an ornament that had special meaning for that specific year.

This has become our annual tradition. We open these on Christmas Eve because we can't wait until Christmas to see what we have picked out. One year I took a picture from our vacation together, cut it down to fit in a small frame, and hung it with red ribbon. The year I got my master's degree my husband wrapped up an ornament from the university I attended. The year we rededicated ourselves to attending church, we unknowingly both gave each other a cross ornament.

As the years go by and we maintain our debt-free Christmas, we will have enough ornaments to trim the entire tree!

Maureen S., Georgia

"Due to your lack of discipline and consistent disregard for your credit limit . . . you have been selected customer of the year!"

16

Dressing the House

Most people refer to getting the house ready for the holidays as decorating, as I did until I developed a fondness for a wonderful carol by Alfred S. Burt called "We'll Dress the House."

Whether you decorate simply or get your home all dressed up for the holidays, there are many ways to do it with grace and elegance, and without spending a lot of money.

Quick as 1, 2, 3

You have little time and even less money to dress the house for the holidays. No problem! Use what you have and concentrate on only three areas.

The front door. Drape a garland intertwined with twinkle lights, hang a wreath, and you're done.

The table. Start with a tablecloth, runner, place mats—anything festive and beautiful. Add a big centerpiece. Set the table with the best things you own. Get out the china and crystal. Go all out and reset after every meal.

The mantel. Remove everything. Start with any kind of greens (pine, magnolia, etc.). Add candles, ornaments, ribbon, cards, and something red—Christmas balls, apples, pomegranates, candles, or fabric.

Note: If you do not have a mantel but you have a staircase, make that your third area of concentration.

O Christmas Tree

As tempting as a pricey, artificial, pre-lit Christmas tree may be, few things about the holidays are as satisfying as a fresh, real Christmas tree. Or as pathetic as a tree that turns brown, loses its needles, and looks like a sorry mess with weeks to go before Christmas morning.

By following the tips below, you have every chance of your tree retaining its fragrance and looking great right through New Year's!

To check the freshness of a tree, gently grasp a branch between your thumb and forefinger and pull it toward you. Very few needles will come off in your hand if the tree is fresh. Shake or bounce the tree on its stump. You should not see an excessive amount of green needles fall to the ground. Some loss of interior brown needles is normal and will occur over the lifetime of a tree.

The best secret for keeping your tree fresh is water, water, water. Once you get your tree, cut ¼ inch off the end and put it immediately into water. Be sure to store your tree in a cool, shaded place out of the sun, such as a covered porch or garage, until you are ready to bring it into the house. Never let your tree run out of water.

If a tree is properly watered, it should stay fresh for two to three weeks. The National Christmas Tree Association does not endorse the use of an additive to the water. Your tree will stay fresh with just plain water.

Within four to six hours of being cut, the tree will form a sap seal over the stump and it will not absorb water. If you forget to make a fresh cut before you set up and decorate your tree, do this: Remove the water from the stand (use a turkey baster). Drill holes into the side of the trunk below the water level. Immediately refill the stand with water, making sure none of the holes are above the water line.

When choosing a tree stand, the most important characteristic is water capacity. A good rule of thumb is one quart for every inch in diameter of a tree's trunk. For example, the average six-foot tree has a trunk with a four-inch diameter, so the tree stand should hold one gallon of water. You should also make sure the stand fits the tree. If it is too big or too small, the tree could tip over. Never trim the sides of a trunk to fit in a stand.

Know your trees. Balsam and Fraser fir are strong and fragrant and hold their needles well. Scotch and white pine are the most popular and least expensive trees. They retain needles through the season and have a good scent, but they can't support many dangling ornaments. Spruce trees have sharp needles, but they're good for holding heavy ornaments.

Buy a living tree to use for the holidays and then plant it in your yard or donate it to a local park or forest once the Christmas season is over. First call your state or local parks and forestry commission to find out where the tree can be planted after the holidays. Other organizations that might enjoy a new tree to add to their landscape are libraries, churches, or schools.

Many states have designated forest areas where you can cut your own tree, provided you have secured a proper permit. Other areas have commercial Christmas tree farms where the kids can help choose and cut the tree. (Typically, it's no bargain, but when combined with a family outing, it might be worth it.)

The National Fire Protection Association tracks fires and their causes. According to their data, real Christmas trees are involved in less than one-tenth of 1 percent of all residential fires. Sensational blazing trees on the evening news are often doused in a flammable liquid or are very old and dried out.

If the nostalgia of a fresh, fragrant tree is not reason enough to go natural, consider these facts:

1. Artificial trees will last for six years in your home (got storage space?) but for centuries in a landfill.
2. Two to three seedlings are planted in the US for every harvested Christmas tree. A total of seventy-three million were planted in 2006 alone.

3. Fifty-nine percent of real Christmas trees harvested are recycled in community programs, providing mulch for landscaping and replenishing the earth's soil.

All Lit Up!

To make your tree sparkle, use lots of miniature lights. To figure out the minimum number you need, multiply the tree's width in feet by eight, then multiply that figure by the tree's height. For example, a four-foot-wide tree that's five feet tall would require 160 lights (4 × 8 = 32 × 5 = 160).

Attach strings of lights from the bottom up. Concentrate them on the bottom two-thirds of the tree and then gradually thin them out toward the top.

If your tree is loaded with a mind-boggling collection of ornaments, limit the lights to one color to help tie everything together. If decorations are sparse, lights in a variety of colors and shapes will help fill things out.

Attach lights first, garlands next, then ornaments. Work from the inside out when hanging ornaments. Put some large, shiny ones on the innermost branches to reflect light and eliminate dark spots.

Trimming Your Tree

It's easy to make clay ornaments, and cheap too. In a saucepan, stir together 2 cups baking soda and 1 cup cornstarch. Add 1¼ cups water. Cook over medium heat, stirring constantly, until mixture is the consistency of moist mashed potatoes. Turn out on a plate and cover with a damp cloth until cool enough to handle. Roll to ¼-inch thickness. Cut shapes with cookie cutters. Use a drinking straw or toothpick to make holes at the top of each ornament. Allow them to dry and harden on a flat surface overnight. Paint, decorate, and then protect them with a shiny glaze.

To brighten the center of a tree, wrap the trunk with foil or garlands of gold tinsel.

Hang your most attractive ornaments at eye level on the outermost branches.

If you don't have a huge collection of ornaments, fill out the tree with Christmas cards, candy canes, ribbons and bows, tinsel, and snowflakes cut from paper doilies. Tiny boxes covered with gift wrap can look surprisingly elegant. Hang gingerbread men, cinnamon sticks tied with bows, and seashells. To add glitter, hang walnuts, pinecones, bay leaves, or blown eggs painted gold or silver.

Experiment with different tree toppers: a china doll dressed in her Sunday best, a big fluffy gold lamé bow, or a bouquet of dried flowers.

Bend medium-gauge wire into the shape of a heart or wreath, then thread with popcorn or cranberries. Top with a bow.

Cut out pictures from magazines, greeting cards, or wrapping paper and glue them to circles of construction paper or cardboard. Attach loops of ribbon to the backs and hang them on the tree.

Help very young children make Christmas ornaments out of red and green pipe cleaners. Twist them into the shape of candy canes, stars, and trees and hang them on the tree or use them to decorate packages.

Cut the bottom out of a plastic berry basket. Cut it into the shape of a snowflake, coat it with glue, and dip it in glitter.

Draw stars and snowflakes in varying sizes on wax paper with white glue that dries hard (such as Elmer's). While the glue is still wet, sprinkle it with glitter. Allow the glue to dry for two days. Then, starting at the points and working in, carefully peel away the wax paper. Hook the stars and snowflakes over the branches of the tree.

String cranberries on thin wire, heavy nylon thread, or fishing line to make garlands.

String popcorn garlands with stale popcorn because it's easier to handle.

Let kids make paper snowflakes out of white or silver paper. Fold paper into eighths and cut designs into all three sides of the wedge. Each one will turn out differently. Attach a ribbon loop to the back or just tuck the snowflakes into the tree branches.

Cover small Styrofoam balls with white glue and attach fresh cranberries. Allow to dry, attach a ribbon, and hang on the tree.

Make paper ornaments out of cardboard. Trace cookie cutter shapes or draw designs freehand. Color the shapes and cut them out. Punch a hole at the top and pull ribbon or string through the hole for hanging.

Any recipe for crisp, rolled cookies can be used to create edible tree decorations. Simply roll and cut the cookie dough as usual, but before baking, use a drinking straw to make a hole near the top of each cookie. (Repeat if hole closes up during baking.) When cookies have cooled, thread ribbon through the holes.

Save plastic, fruit-shaped lemon- and lime-juice squeeze bottles. Rinse out the containers and let them dry. Thread a six-inch piece of yarn or ribbon through the loop in the lid (or if there is no loop, tie the yarn around the cap) and hang on the Christmas tree.

Create a gift tree. You'll need small boxes of all sizes and shapes (empty Jell-O boxes are perfect), wrapping paper, and coordinating curling ribbon. Depending on the size of your tree, you'll need thirty to fifty small, empty containers. Wrap each with paper and curling ribbon. Tie the "gifts" to the tree, placing the small ones at the top and the larger ones at the bottom. You can use different patterns of wrapping paper or wrap every gift in the same paper and ribbon. This is especially dramatic with gold or silver foil packages and small white lights.

Thread polystyrene peanuts for garlands.

Save all the toys your kids receive during the year with fast-food meals and use them to decorate a small artificial tree just for the kids. Tie the toys on with ribbons, but allow the kids to take off the toys and play with them. This will help make your fancy tree with fragile decorations a little less tempting.

Place star, tree, or other holiday stickers back-to-back along a wire or ribbon. Wind it like garland through the branches of the tree.

Tie bows all over the tree.

Instead of a traditional evergreen tree, bring a potted tree in from the garden or terrace for the holidays, or decorate an indoor plant or tree with small ornaments. Small red ribbons on a Norfolk pine, masses of white lights on a ficus, or any plant covered with colorful popcorn and cranberry garlands can be very festive.

Decorate a tiny live tree with fruit ornaments and ribbon and set it on the kitchen table or countertop.

After the tree is undecorated and ready to be thrown out, strip off all the needles. (Make sure you wear gloves.) Then put them into a pillow slip and cover it with a pretty pillow cover. The scent will last all year and will keep the spirit and anticipation of Christmas alive.

House Dressing

Have you ever noticed that our eyes become mercifully selective once our homes are dressed for the holidays? The slightly worn carpet and tired sofa seem to disappear when upstaged by even the simplest decorations.

Likely, you already have more than enough materials in your drawers, attic, and yard to turn your home into a warm and attractive setting for a holiday celebration. What you need are some great idea starters. And I've got some great ones for you.

Candles are a simple and natural way to decorate for Christmas. If all you have are pine-tree greenery and candles, you have all you need. Use candles lavishly and light them as often as possible. Nothing will turn your home into a softer, more beautiful place faster than candles. Never, ever leave candles burning unattended. If you leave the room, always extinguish open flames before you go.

Line your walkways, driveway, or other areas on your property with luminaries made from paper bags filled with two inches of sand and a votive candle in the center.

Make luminaries that can be kept from year to year. Rinse out a tin can and pinch all rough edges flat and smooth. Fill the can with water and freeze. When the ice is solid, remove the can from the freezer. Using a permanent marker, draw designs around the sides of the can, making sure the design does not come within one inch of the bottom. Place the can on its side on a towel so it won't slip. With a nail and hammer, punch holes along the design lines you've drawn. Leave about a half inch or so between each punch. Then allow the ice to melt and drain. Place a votive candle in each can and line your walkway. Light your luminaries every night during the holidays.

Little ones will believe Santa was actually in their home if you make boot prints with baking soda. Just dampen the bottom of a pair of boots, dip them into baking soda, and make tracks leading from the chimney to the tree and then to the cookies and milk. Make sure the cookies and milk are properly consumed. The baking soda will vacuum up easily.

Display an assortment of great family Christmas pictures from years past in a special photo album or in a location where your family and guests can enjoy them.

Decoupage a serving tray with last year's Christmas cards and set it on your coffee table.

Make golden angels by gluing silk-leaf wings and a hazelnut head to a pinecone, then spraying them with metallic paint. If you don't have silk leaves, cut leaf shapes from cardboard.

Buy a big candle for the dinner table. Light it every night at dinner during the holidays.

Make miniature Christmas trees for a great holiday family activity. Glue the wide ends of sugar ice-cream cones to a large sheet of cardboard. Spread green icing over the cones and then decorate them with assorted candies such as M&Ms, gumdrops, and Life Savers. Let the kids come up with new decorating ideas for the "family forest."

For an instant table dress-up, heap shiny Christmas balls of all sizes in an elegant glass bowl. Place the bowl near candles and allow the light to bounce off all the shiny surfaces of the centerpiece.

Wrap a tinsel garland around the bedroom or bathroom mirror.

Arrange poinsettias in a bare corner and tie big, bright bows around the pots.

Don't know how to fill the stockings hanging by the chimney with care? Fill them with stockings! Everyone loves argyles, tube socks, running socks, or knee highs. Stockings filled with stockings are fun and practical.

Instead of decorating the outside of your home to please your kids, decorate each child's room to get them excited about the holidays. Help your children make red and green paper chains from construction paper to hang all over their rooms. Not only is this activity less time-consuming than attempting a big exterior display, but it may also establish a special tradition your children will not forget. Plus, you won't have to say "Time for bed!" twice when your child can nestle among the enchanting lights of his or her very own bedside boughs.

Wrap your child's bedroom door with wrapping paper to transform it into a giant package.

Place white twinkle lights on your large houseplants.

Hang mistletoe in every single doorway of your house.

Frosted fruits are a delicious-looking centerpiece and are simple to make. Simmer apple jelly with a little water, let it cool, then brush it over fruit. Roll the fruit in granulated sugar to coat.

Put Christmas lights and a small wreath on the dog's house.

Gold, one of the gifts the wise men carried to Bethlehem, is a symbol of generosity. For a truly glittering Christmas, recycle miniature pumpkins and squash left from Halloween and Thanksgiving and spray them with gold paint. Place them throughout the house or use them in centerpieces, garlands, and topiaries. Gild walnuts, pinecones, bay leaves, dried flowers, apples, pomegranates, pineapples, lemons, and grapes. Wear gloves, a dust mask, and glasses or goggles when spraying.

For just the price of wrapping paper and ribbon, you can decorate your entire home in a truly spectacular way. Gift wrap all the framed pictures and paintings on your walls. The effect is stunning. Tip: Wrap only the fronts and sides and you'll use less paper.

Decorate the guest bath by wrapping a tissue box like a gift.

Sew small brass jingle bells along the hem of a tablecloth.

Increase the effectiveness of votive candles by placing them on squares of mirrored glass.

Lay sprays of evergreens on the mantelpiece, thread a string of white lights (on green wire) through them, and nestle some of your collectibles or Christmas balls amid the greens. If you have no evergreen in your yard, find a friend or neighbor who will allow you to clip some of theirs.

Cover the mantel or a wide windowsill with a bed of Spanish moss. Tuck in ivy, holly, pinecones, and a few gilded nuts and fruits.

Pile red apples on a bed of evergreen and tuck in some tiny Christmas balls.

Drape a long rope of greens (tied together with narrow-gauge wire) over the front door. Attach a red velvet or satin bow in the middle and weave matching ribbon through the garland like a streamer. As a finishing touch, place a poinsettia plant on each side of the doorway.

Hang your holiday wreath on a four-inch-wide silk ribbon on a mirror in your entryway or over the mantelpiece.

Fill a basket with large pinecones interspersed with clusters of delicate baby's breath. Thread tiny white lights throughout, hiding the wires under the pinecones.

Hang extra mirrors around the house during the holidays to add to the glow and to multiply the special effects of your decorations.

Wind strands of white Christmas lights and greens around the banister. Add large plaid bows.

Place a poinsettia or flowering plant on every step of a staircase to peek through the banister.

Tape, tie, or staple Christmas cards to ribbon streamers to hang for display.

Put several different sizes of poinsettia plants in cache pots or baskets and add trailing ivy.

If the kids' rooms, basement, or spare rooms are always a mess, just close the doors and hang wreaths on them.

Fill a glass container with holiday candy and top with a lid or a circle of gift wrap or foil. Tie with ribbon and set on a table.

Decorate doors with Christmas trees cut from foam board. Pin, tape, or glue on bright ornaments and garlands of beads.

Paint a bright red bow on a doormat. Add a painted tag with the family's name.

Make a gumdrop wreath. Either buy a Styrofoam wreath or cut one out. Use toothpicks or stiff wire to attach red, white, and green gumdrops to the wreath or use multicolored ones to resemble Christmas tree lights. Top off the wreath with a big bow.

Fill a large glass bowl three-quarters full of water. Place small, flat-bottomed candles such as tea lights in aluminum foil muffin tin liners and gently set them afloat in the water. Light them carefully and enjoy.

Use crystal or cut-glass bowls of different sizes to make a holiday arrangement. Fill one bowl with Christmas balls—either place them upside down to hide the hangers or tie a small bow on each. (This is a great way to use ornaments that are damaged.) In another bowl, combine fresh fruit with evergreens. In a third bowl, add holiday-scented handmade or purchased potpourri. Place votive candles in small bowls.

Try a wreath centerpiece. Core five apples, making a two-inch-deep hole at the center of each to hold a candle. Lay a wire wreath frame on a flat surface and attach the evenly spaced cored apples with a glue gun. Arrange cedar, spruce, and holly sprigs in one direction along the wreath and wrap in place with fine wire. Attach small pinecones with a glue gun and insert tall, tapered candles in the apples.

Create a fruit centerpiece. Tie individual oranges (lemons, limes, or apples will also work) with ribbon and then stack them into a tree shape on a pedestal plate.

Set out pretty containers of pine, evergreen, or cinnamon potpourri in every room.

Keep plenty of throws and afghans around the living room. They look great and invite people to curl up and get cozy.

Display all your holiday cards so they add to your home's decor. Find a piece of string that is just a bit longer than your front window and attach the ends to either side at the top of the window. Hang the cards from the string by folding them over the string so the front of the cards face out. Once full, the string will drape ever so slightly to give a beautiful valance effect across the top of the window.

Hang wreaths on the inside, as well as the outside, of your doors.

Make pomander balls. Buy a supply of whole cloves (they're expensive at the supermarket; try a health food store that sells spices in bulk) and some oranges. Insert the cloves into the oranges (you can poke holes in the rind using a small knitting needle). Wrap the pomanders with red ribbon and hang them around the house.

Rather than buying new decorations, refurbish old ones. Give life to a wreath by adding fresh ribbon. Glue glitter on faded ornaments. Make it a personal creative challenge to decorate with only those things you already have in the home.

Go back to old standards such as popcorn and cranberry garlands and construction-paper chains.

Outdoors

If you're fresh out of oversized Santas for the yard and have no snow for snowmen, make a family of broom people to warm the hearts of passersby. Stick the broom handles into the lawn. Cut white circles for eyes from felt or white cardboard and draw black dots in the centers for the pupils. Glue these eyes to the bristle part of the brooms. Top with real hats and ear muffs; tie scarves around the handles. Let your imagination go wild, not your pocketbook.

Tie outdoor lights to trees and posts with strips cut from the legs of old pantyhose.

Surround window frames with greens and strings of outdoor lights.

Hang ornaments cut from foil pie plates on a tree or bush near the house and watch them sparkle.

When our son was only three, we wanted to make sure he grew up knowing the reason we celebrate Christmas—Jesus' birthday. His response? "Where's the cake?" This sent me scrambling to see if I had any cake mix, as it was Christmas Eve and most stores were already closing for the holiday. All I had was a carrot cake mix, so that is what we made.

To this day, not only do we make a birthday cake for Jesus each Christmas Eve, but it has to be a carrot cake. Our son, much older now, does all the decorating, and it is fun to watch how his creativity grows with each passing year.

Jeanette L., email

We make a game of hiding Mary and Joseph (as they are traveling the long journey to Bethlehem) at night when the children are sleeping. Every morning the kids have to find them. On Christmas morning, they are in the stable with Jesus in the manger. This game helps keep the holidays fun, and the anticipation builds for the arrival of Jesus.

Pat C., email

The year was 1991. My favorite book in the world was and still is How the Grinch Stole Christmas. Macy's was selling a stuffed Grinch for five dollars with every fifty-dollar purchase. My dad didn't have much money, and he couldn't afford to spend the fifty dollars, but he really wanted me to have the Grinch as a special present. For days he went to Macy's and asked customers with shopping bags if they had gotten their five-dollar Grinch—and if not, could they turn in their receipts so he could get the Grinch for his daughter. He finally found a customer who was willing to help him. It was a wonderful surprise and a great story. The Grinch still sits on my bed to this day. Now the story has even more meaning for my son, who is quite taken with my very own Grinch.

Jennifer G., email

"I don't know why these people can't just relax and let me do my job. I can do in one night what they spend all year trying to get done!"

17

Holiday Entertaining

Inviting friends and family to your home during the holidays doesn't have to end up costing a fortune. The key to effective entertaining is to remember that your guests are far more interested in spending time with you than seeing you fret and fume as you attempt to pull off the event of the century.

Over the years I have collected many tips and tricks for how to do things better and cheaper when it comes to holiday entertaining. And my best lessons came as a result of discovering what doesn't work.

If there is one thing I've learned that rises to the top of things you need to know, it is this: above all, relax. What's really important is that you are free to enjoy your guests enjoying themselves.

Planning and Preparation

Instead of everyone in your circle of friends hosting a separate holiday party, make plans to have a progressive dinner. Have beverages and hors d'oeuvres at the first home, appetizers or soup at the second, main course at the next, and dessert and coffee at the last. It's an enjoyable way to share the burden—and the glory—and you get to see everyone's holiday decorations too.

To cut back on entertaining costs, hold a joint party with a friend or relative and split the labor, as well as the expense. Or have a caroling party and just serve cookies and hot drinks.

Instead of a full-fledged dinner party, host an adults-only coffee party where each guest contributes a dessert. This way everyone makes something really special instead of one person being up to her armpits in preparation and hosting.

Be realistic about how much you can do. You don't have to see everyone between Thanksgiving and New Year's, for example. Save some get-togethers until after the holidays, and you'll have something to look forward to. The house will still look great, and you won't feel as rushed.

If you're having two holiday parties at your home, schedule them back-to-back. Serve an identical (or at least similar) menu. It takes the same amount of time to make a double batch. Bonus: All your serving pieces will be out, and your home will be clean.

Use Christmas stickers or fancy stamps to dress up plain notepaper for invitations or thank-you cards.

When guests ask to bring something, let them. But be specific about what you need so you don't end up with too much of one thing.

Copy your favorite cookie recipe on a card, wrap colorful cellophane around a couple of freshly baked samples, and tie everything with a bright red ribbon. Give one to each guest as a favor.

Plan to keep one room sparkling clean just for visitors, and don't let anyone in it before you have guests.

Be prepared for surprise guests and keep some generic gifts (candy or comics for kids, candles or calendars for adults) at the ready. Use color-coded wrap, stickers, or ribbon to help match the gift to the recipient.

Memorize the ten-minute rescue. The phone rings. Surprise! Long-lost friends will be at your front door in ten minutes. You have no time to clean the house or even to panic. Instead, move into high gear with this ten-minute rescue:

1. Set a small pan of water over medium heat. Add spices such as cinnamon, allspice, and cloves, and heat.
2. Grab a box or grocery bag and clear all coffee tables, end tables, and kitchen counters into it. Stash it in a closet.

3. Gather all bathroom clutter and deposit it in the tub or shower and draw the curtain.

4. Pull out a special basket (prepared ahead of time and stashed under the sink) with a couple of pretty holiday towels and guest soaps tucked in it and place it on the vanity.

5. Clean all flat surfaces you cleared with furniture polish or all-purpose cleaner.

6. Starting at the front door, vacuum the visible areas.

7. Light candles and the fireplace. Switch on the stereo and turn down the lights. Ta-da!

Decorating the Table

If you have a pretty table, let it show. Make simple place mats by cutting holiday fabric into rectangles and ironing on a hem with fusible webbing.

If you don't have adequate matching flatware and dishes for a large group—most people don't—don't be afraid to mix and match. Just tie everything together with matching napkins.

Create a simple centerpiece. Trail greens or ivy down the center of the table, then add fresh fruit or holly for color and craft-store pearls for sparkle.

Dress up your napkins by tying each with a ribbon and a small bell.

Put a small, framed photograph of each person at his or her place instead of traditional place cards.

Set the table the day before with everything (including platters) to make sure it all fits and looks attractive. Cover with a clean sheet to keep dust-free.

Food

When you're hosting a party, arrange the appetizers, snacks, and beverages on several tables. This keeps everybody circulating instead of gathered at one spot where the food is. You can also ask guests who seem a little shy to pass around appetizers; it helps them break the ice.

Make an ice ring for your punch bowl with fruit juice or sherbet instead of water. It looks pretty, and it won't water down the punch as it melts.

Never serve red punch. It stains carpeting.

Use unusual serving dishes. Put crudités in brightly colored mugs or bread in a shiny metal colander.

Garnish platters with Christmas colors. Arrange cherry tomatoes and mint leaves or fresh dill and sliced red peppers around the edge.

Display your holiday cookies in a special way. Arrange them on colorful tissue paper or in pretty baskets lined with Christmas fabric.

Be realistic about the menu. Don't choose recipes that are too elaborate or require last-minute preparation. If you have time to make only one blowout course, make it dessert because that's the last impression everyone will take home with them.

Don't be afraid to use prepared foods. Put a store-bought appetizer on your finest china, garnish it with herbs, and no one will know the difference, or care.

Do as much work in advance as you can. Bake and freeze desserts and side dishes in microwavable containers.

Organize your refrigerator for easy access to the food you'll be using most. Put all the appetizer or salad supplies together in a container or on a tray, labeled and ready to use.

If you are having a large group, consider a buffet. Just be sure to choose dishes that can be served at room temperature and will still look good after sitting out for an hour or so.

Several years ago, when the kids were still small, we started a tradition by putting a little envelope way up in the Christmas tree. When all the presents had been opened and the excitement of the morning began to die down, we all lounged around the living room. My ten-year-old daughter suddenly spied the little paper way up in the tree.

"Daddy, what's that?" she asked.

With a shrug, he picked it out of the tree and handed it to her and her eight-year-old brother. Inside the envelope was a single clue that sent both of them on a hunt to find the prize.

This has turned into a tradition we call The Hunt. The "big prize" was at the end of The Hunt—something fairly insignificant for each child. The fun was following the clues and having to look high and low, inside and out.

I learned how much this had become a part of our lives one year when I had the nerve to forget to include The Hunt in our Christmas morning. The kids were visibly disappointed—let down because they had expected another round of clues and laughter as they worked together on their quest. Later that Christmas morning, I found them cutting up strips of paper and making up clues for each other to go on their own Christmas hunt.

After that year, they started dropping hints in mid-November for their not-so-bright mom. Comments like, "I sure hope we get to go on The Hunt this year," or "It doesn't really matter what we find at the end; I just really want to go on The Hunt!" Okay, okay, I get it!

They are teenagers now, and the tradition lives on. When I asked them what they liked best and least about our Christmas this year, they both quickly said they still like The Hunt the best.

Karen C., email

"So . . . that means if I buy four, it won't cost anything?"

18

Family Fun

Look ahead twenty years. You're gathered around the table with your children, grandchildren—perhaps even some great-grandchildren.

Conversation turns to Christmases past. What will your children tell their kids they loved most about that long-ago Christmas? Seeing Mom spend days on end cleaning the house so Grandma would be impressed? Will they even remember how many gifts they received or even those they gave?

Probably not.

Your children will remember the fun family times. It is sobering to think that every day you are participating in the creation of your children's childhood memories. If you still have time to do something about those memories, don't miss the opportunity.

Feeling a little blue because your nest is empty this year? Invite a family with young children to a tree-trimming party.

If the onslaught of relatives and activities leaves you taking care of everyone but yourself, it may be time to change your holiday habits. Instead of accepting every invitation, take a day—or a few hours—and do something special with your family. Watch a movie, bake a batch of cookies—anything you want to do for a change.

Start a new tradition. Even though Santa fills all the stockings on Christmas Eve, leave them hanging full and untouched until New Year's Day. This helps to relieve the feeling of overdose on Christmas morning and is a nice way to celebrate the New Year.

Let your kids turn one of your windows into a holiday canvas. Mix powdered tempera paints (available at an art supply store or craft store) with clear dishwashing liquid until you have the creamy consistency of house paint. If you have premixed tempera paint, stir in a bit of the dish soap. Use individual plastic containers (margarine tubs are perfect) to mix the colors. Cover the window sash with masking tape, and spread newspaper around the surrounding area. Then let the window artists take it away. If you're using a large picture window, help the kids design a mural. Dad and Mom can get into the act by painting the hard-to-reach areas. Windows with individual panes offer a great opportunity for a Christmas montage of a snowflake, a bell, a candy cane, a Christmas tree—one design per pane. When it's completely dry, the paint will come off easily—just wipe with a dry paper towel.

While sitting around the fire one cold winter evening, take turns writing down past events you'd like to forget, then toss them into the fireplace.

Take extra time off work while the kids are out of school for the holidays.

Make special holiday place mats with your kids. All you need is a box of crayons and light-colored vinyl place mats. Help the kids draw holiday designs and write their name. After the holidays, simply wipe the mats clean with a good all-purpose liquid cleaner. Some traces of color may remain, so make sure you don't use your very best place mats.

Take an evening for the whole family to prepare and decorate luminaries (see chapter 16).

Take the family to see a small-town Christmas parade.

Prior to Thanksgiving Day, deliver a ticket to each family member and instruct them to write their current interests, hobbies, and

Christmas gift requests. As you sit around the table, have each person read what's on his or her list. Or have everyone put their list into a hat so that drawing names now comes with an instant gift idea list.

Adopt a needy family for the holidays. Make a special shopping trip or have a gift-making session when each member of your family buys or creates a present for the person in the adopted family who is closest to their age.

Volunteer as a family to work in a soup kitchen or homeless shelter.

Take a basket of holiday goodies to your local fire or police station.

Attach a wreath and big red bow to the front grill of the family car. Hang a fun ornament from the rearview mirror.

Tie jingle bells to everyone's sneakers and go caroling to your neighbors' homes. Or just take a walk through the mall. Oh, what fun.

Before going to bed on Christmas Eve, turn out all the lights and light lots of candles. Read the second chapter of Luke from the Bible and sing "Silent Night."

Instead of reading the usual bedtime stories during the month of December, read to your children about Christmas customs in other countries, as well as other wonderful holiday stories available at your local library or online. Find stories that come from the countries that represent your children's heritage.

One night a week during the holiday season, eat dinner by the light of the Christmas tree. Teach the family to say "Merry Christmas" in the language of the family's origin.

If you have relatives living far away, make a video of your family decorating the house and trimming the tree. Send it to them to enjoy on Christmas Day.

Get out the board games and have an ongoing family tournament during December.

If you take your kids to see Santa, save time and aggravation waiting in long lines by staying away from overcrowded malls. Instead, check smaller department stores or neighborhood centers.

If Santa's booth allows you to take your own photographs (most do, but be sure to inquire ahead of time), take your own camera when your kids visit with the old gent. Instead of ordering duplicates of the photo, copy it yourself on your home computer or drop into a quick-print place and have colored photocopy enlargements made for about one dollar each.

Caroling spreads cheer throughout your neighborhood. Bring a thermos of hot cocoa to keep everyone warm.

Make a wreath from greenery you find in your own backyard and let the children decorate it.

Bake Christmas cookies for your child's class at school. To save time, make the slice-and-bake variety and decorate them with ready-made frosting.

On the last day of school before Christmas vacation, tie red and green balloons to the mailbox to welcome your children home.

Buy a large white candle (3 x 8 inches is ideal). Starting at the top, carefully carve twenty-five evenly spaced horizontal stripes around the candle with the point of a knife. At a designated time each day (dinnertime or bedtime), starting on December 1, light the candle and decide on something you're thankful for as a family. Allow the advent candle to burn down one stripe each night until Christmas.

Start a giant jigsaw puzzle at the beginning of the season. The goal is to be finished by Christmas Day. Keep it out on a table in a well-lit area so anyone can work on it whenever they want.

Reserve opening the day's Christmas cards until dinnertime. Read the messages aloud and remind the kids how the family knows these people.

Attend a Christmas pageant at your elementary school, even if you do not have children in the school.

If you are single, getting together with a group of friends who are also single is a great way to celebrate Christmas. How about hosting a work party where everyone bakes cookies, prepares their cards, and wraps gifts? Some activities are a lot more fun when done in a group. The evening could end with an ornament swap.

If you find it nearly impossible to gather together all of your married children and their families on Christmas Eve or Christmas Day, consider a new tradition of spending the day after Christmas together. This will give you one more day to prepare, and because this is a day typically free from other intrusions, you'll be able to spend a more relaxed time together.

Take a nighttime walk in your neighborhood to enjoy the holiday lights. It's fun to see decorations up close and personal.

Go to a recital at a local church. Many choirs perform Handel's *Messiah* and other seasonal favorites.

Plan a cookie-decorating event with your kids. Bake the cookies early in the day. At party time, set out various toppings and icings. If you've invited friends, let each child take home a batch of goodies.

If you have so many in attendance at your Christmas dinner that you must have two tables or more, have everyone get up and exchange places between dinner and dessert to mix things up and to give everyone a chance to be together.

On New Year's Eve, ask each family member to light a candle and think about the things that happened in the past year for which they are most thankful.

Save a piece of the Christmas tree's trunk to burn as next year's Yule log. Tell the family the legend behind the Yule log. Long ago, people brought home the largest log they could find, usually ash in England or birch in Scotland. They decorated it with a sprig of holly, placed it in the fireplace, and lit it with a piece of the log saved from the previous year. It was hoped that it would burn throughout the twelve days of Christmas. In many households, the lady of the house kept the kindling piece under her pillow. It was thought that this provided year-round protection against fire. If you don't have a fireplace, bring home a festive cake in the shape of a Yule log for Christmas Eve to share with the whole family—or take on a challenge and make a Bûche de Noël yourself.

Give your family a post-Christmas treat by celebrating Twelfth Night on January 6. Also known as the Feast of Epiphany, this Victorian tradition celebrates the day the three wise men arrived in Bethlehem with their gifts for the Christ child. Children are given three gifts from the magi before a gala dinner. Afterward, a Twelfth Night cake decorated with figures of kings is served. The child who receives the piece containing the silver coin baked into it becomes "king" or "queen" of the family for the whole year!

Make a "Pin the Red Nose on Rudolph" game board. Draw Rudolph's head on a big sheet of poster board and cut red noses out of construction paper. Use loops of tape to attach the nose.

Instead of sending holiday cards to your neighbors, start a new tradition. Organize "The Bentley Street Christmas Book" (or whatever the name of your street or neighborhood). Begin a story (fictional) in a notebook, attach a routing slip with the name of each family on your street, and then send it around the neighborhood with directions for each family to add a sentence or paragraph. When the story comes back to your family, add an appropriate ending. Edit as necessary, print out the story on your computer, and assemble it into a simple book, one for each family that contributed. Have a neighborhood get-together and read the crazy tale. This will bond your neighbors and promote goodwill all through the year.

Call your local post office to see if they collect letters kids have written to Santa. If they do, have your children pick some out. Then select gifts, wrap them, and send them off anonymously. This experience helps teach kids the joy of giving without expecting something in return.

Carve out a quiet hour or two for a storytelling party with the entire family. Read classic Christmas stories aloud.

Every Christmas Eve, have your children leave some of their gently used toys near the fireplace for Santa to take to children who don't have any toys. Once the kids are asleep, hide the toys so you can deliver them to a worthy charity later.

Get the family together during the week after Christmas. Review your holiday plan and the goals you met. Ask everyone what they liked best and least about the holidays and what they'd like to do differently next year. Take notes.

Each year my sisters, cousins, and friends get together for a "wrap party." We all bring the gifts we need wrapped, our supplies, and a potluck dish. We gather the weekend before Christmas and have a ball! Those who are "wrapping challenged" have others there who enjoy wrapping to help them out. We all get a chance to catch up, it encourages all of us to get the shopping done on time, and it saves us all from last-minute wrapping.

          Madge H., email

Our children never let us forget their favorite family tradition. We allow them to open their Christmas presents before Christmas. This way they have time to enjoy our gifts before receiving their other Christmas gifts from extended family. It works like this. After school on the Friday before Christmas, we have our usual pizza-night dinner. Then we slip into pajamas and head to the living room. We read the Christmas story from the Bible, open presents, stay up late watching Christmas movies, and then (their favorite part) sleep by the Christmas tree. In the morning, we have breakfast in our pajamas, and the kids play with their new things. The kids love it.

          Jennifer K., email

After lunch on Christmas day, we go to a nearby nursing home to bring homemade cards from my daughter's class, some cookies, and small gifts to the elderly who may not have family to bring them home or visit them. It is a wonderful tradition, and we get as much, if not more, out of it as the residents. My favorite memory was passing by the pay phone and seeing a lady with her card telling the person on the other end of the line how this sweet child came in to wish her a Merry Christmas and gave her a gift. It warmed my heart.

Anne S., email

Conclusion

It was an unusual interview. The woman explained she was writing an article for a national magazine on clever ways to put more joy into the holidays. Because I've written a lot on this subject, she called hoping I would help her with the story. I knew that I could.

In my typical, overly helpful manner, I proceeded to pitch to her one marvelous holiday cost-cutting idea after another—some of them principle-based, others uniquely practical.

It didn't take long for me to realize that something wasn't right. One after another, my ideas landed with a thud. She didn't like them at all. And that's when she made a comment that effectively brought the interview to a screeching halt.

She called me a grinch.

Now, she didn't actually come right out and say, "You grinch!" She said that if she wrote an article encouraging the unthinkable practices of not incurring debt, buying fewer gifts, or cutting back in any way, her readers would think she'd interviewed that old you-know-who himself.

While she suggested my ideas would take all the fun and joy out of the season, she assured me it was nothing personal. But still, she called me a grinch.

Not being one who can easily let things go, I had to get to the bottom of this. I had to find out if what she suggested about me was in any way true. In my zeal to encourage people to take back control of Christmas from the locked jaws of commercialism, had I taken on a striking resemblance to that cranky old holiday grump, the Grinch?

I was quite certain I knew where to find out. And sure enough, right there on the shelf between *Horton Hears a Who* and *Hunches in Bunches* I found it—that familiar bright-red storybook: *How the Grinch Stole Christmas!*

It seems that for fifty-three years the Grinch has lived in a cave just north of Who-ville. He's an ornery old soul with a heart two sizes too small. The Grinch detests the holiday celebrations down in Who-ville. So he devises a plan.

He steals all their presents and every last decoration. He hauls all the loot to the top of Mount Crumpit, where he prepares to—you guessed it—dump it.

He thinks his task is complete. All the noise, the joy, and the love—even the smallest hint of the season—are gone forever.

But then he hears a sound. It's not sobbing but singing! The Whos are celebrating with no presents at all.

I sat there recalling why I love this story so much. And I admit it—I felt delightfully smug. My interviewer was way off base. I'm not the grinch in her story. I didn't steal the joy. Her grinches are consumerism, overindulgence, and overdoing—the attitudes that insist Christmas is something we can find in a store, catalog, outlet, or on the internet.

If you've noticed the joy of the season is missing from your life—that no matter how hard you try, something's just not right—maybe those grinches are to blame. Maybe it's time to let them know they've lost their power.

Authentic joy comes not from all the outside trappings but from our hearts. It comes from the story of the birth of a small baby who would become our Savior—from that love, which can fill our lives with giddy joy.

And now we come to the close of our journey to a debt-proof Christmas.

America's beloved poet Robert Frost expressed the significance of decisions and the wisdom to decide in this much-loved poem:

The Road Not Taken

Two roads diverged in a yellow wood,
And sorry I could not travel both
And be one traveler, long I stood
And looked down one as far as I could
To where it bent in the undergrowth;

Then took the other, as just as fair,
And having perhaps the better claim,
Because it was grassy and wanted wear;
Though as for that the passing there
Had worn them really about the same,

And both that morning equally lay
In leaves no step had trodden black.
Oh, I kept the first for another day!
Yet knowing how way leads on to way,
I doubted if I should ever come back.

I shall be telling this with a sigh
Somewhere ages and ages hence:
Two roads diverged in a wood, and I—
I took the one less traveled by,
And that has made all the difference.

Robert Frost (1874–1963)

Life is a series of forks in the road. One decision leads to another. Is it a wise decision or one that will be destructive? Does it lead to higher ground or a valley of despair? Does it set us up for something better and more fulfilling? Or does it lead to eventual defeat, steady decline, and self-destruction?

So here we stand at yet another fork in the road. One path is posted "debt-free." It's the less-traveled, slower route, narrow and uphill. But at the destination waits joy, simplicity, satisfaction, and a trophy engraved "paid in full."

The other road is "convenience," a very tempting, ultramodern highway paved with easy credit. Taking this high-tech option means effortless travel. But holiday overindulgence, dissatisfaction, and stress leave many travelers filled with guilt, regret, and fear. There is no trophy for reaching this destination, only a miserable monthly reminder of the high cost of convenience. Which road will you take? That decision will make all the difference.

May this and every Christmas for you and your family be one of peace and joy.

Notes

Chapter 6: Holiday Dilemmas

1. National Retail Federation 2011 Holiday Survival Kit, www.nrf.com/modules .php?name=Pages&sp_id=1487.

2. http://blog.checkadvantage.com/2011/02/11/debt-rises-in-december/.

3. Bill McKibben, *Hundred Dollar Holiday* (New York: Simon & Schuster, 1998), 43.

Chapter 7: The Gentle Art of Gift-Giving

4. Giving statistics compiled by the U.S. Department of the Interior dated October 17, 2011, www.nps.gov/partnerships/fundraising_individuals_statistics.htm.

5. Julie Steenhuysen, "Brain Gets Thrill from Charity: Study," Reuters, June 14, 2007, www.reuters.com/article/2007/06/14/us-brain-altruism-idUSN1418520820070614.

Chapter 8: Finding the Bargains

6. "Signs Indicate Weak 2010 Winter Holiday Sales," www.towergroup.com/ research/news/news.htm?newsid=5500 and "Don't Be 'Breakage'—8 Tips to Avoid Losing Gift Card Value," www.creditcards.com/credit-card-news/8-tips-losing-gift-card-funds-breakage-spillage-1271.php.

7. National Retail Federation, "Return Fraud to Cost Retailers $3.7 Billion This Holiday Season," www.nrf.com/modules.php?name=News&op=viewlive&sp_id =1024.

8. www.smartbargains.com/Promo/Help/Help-Return-Policy.aspx?t=Home ...rtrn-link.#Damaged.

Chapter 13: Traditions Are the Glue That Holds Us Together

9. Jo Robinson and Jean C. Staeheli, *Unplug the Christmas Machine: A Complete Guide to Putting Love and Joy Back into the Season* (New York: William Morrow Paperbacks, 1991), 51.

Index

Recipes Index

Book Mary to speak at your next event

Over the past twenty years Mary has spoken at live events, conferences, seminars, and retreats across the United States and around the world. Here's what others are saying about Mary:

"We love when Mary comes to IWU, she always relates so well to our students."
—Chapel speaker and business school guest lecturer, 2000, 2001, 2005, 2009, and 2011, Indiana Wesleyan University

"Thank you, Mary, for speaking at the 2008 Biennial Conference for Women. Your presentation was outstanding!"
—Biennial Conference for Women, 2008, University of Illinois Urbana-Champaign

"The key and strength of Mary's message is that people come away thinking they could actually do what she teaches! This is the very exciting part of her writing and speaking ministry."
—Pastors and Spouses Retreat, 2010, Canadian Conference of MB Churches

To book Mary or learn more about her, contact:

Cathy Hollenbeck
PO Box 2099
Paramount, CA   90723
(562) 630-6472
Cathy@DebtProofLiving.com
www.DebtProofLiving.com

What Is Debt-Proof Living?

It's a great big wonderful website offering help and hope to anyone who wants to learn how to manage their money more effectively. If you want to get out of debt—or stay out—and learn how to live below your means, Debt-Proof Living is the place to be. It encompasses many elements:

A lifestyle

Debt-proof living is a way of life where you spend less than you earn; you give and save consistently; your financial decisions are purposeful; you work toward your goals by following a specific plan.

A system of personal money management

Debt-proof living is a specific method that makes it possible to debt-proof your life.

A newsletter

In continuous publication since 1992, DPL newsletter is now published in an online format available to all members of this website.

A website

DebtProofLiving.com is the home of the debt-proof living brand. It is primarily a member-only website with features ranging from money management tools, articles, resources, community forums, consumer tips, recipes, and more.

Visit **www.DebtProofLiving.com** today!

These 7 simple rules will change your life!

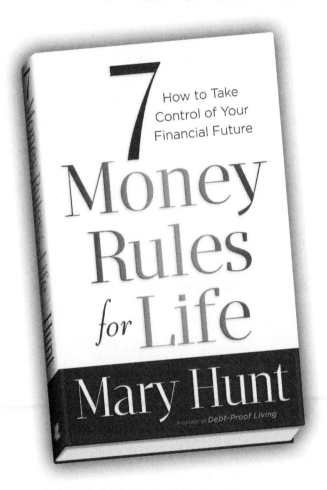

These days most of us need some help managing our money. Mary Hunt's simple rules will move you from financial uncertainty to financial confidence!

Teach your kids to have a healthy relationship with money and build a strong financial future.*

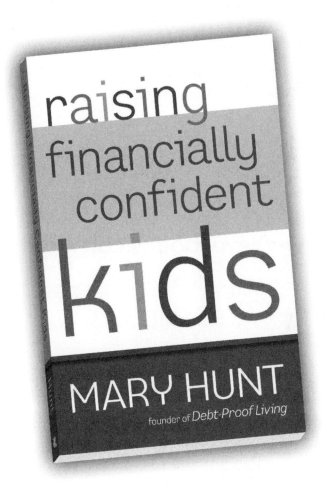

*Even if you still have a lot to learn.

Mary Hunt can show you how.

Be the First
to Hear about
Other New Books
from Revell!

Sign up for announcements about
new and upcoming titles at

www.revellbooks.com/signup

Follow us on **twitter**
RevellBooks

Join us on **facebook**
Revell

Don't miss out on our great reads!

Revell
a division of Baker Publishing Group
www.RevellBooks.com